Organic Foods

Organic Foods

JENNIFER MACKAY

LUCENT BOOKS

A part of Gale, Cengage Learning

GALE
CENGAGE Learning·

Farmington Hills, Mich • San Francisco • New York • Waterville, Maine
Meriden, Conn • Mason, Ohio • Chicago

LIBRARY OF CONGRESS CATALOGING-IN-PUBLICATION DATA

MacKay, Jennifer, author.
  Organic foods / by Jennifer MacKay.
     pages cm. -- (Nutrition and health)
  Includes bibliographical references and index.
  ISBN 978-1-4205-1243-4 (hardcover)
  1. Organic farming. 2. Natural foods. I. Title. II. Series: Nutrition & health (Lucent Books)
  S605.5.M3223 2015
  631.5'84--dc23
                                    2014043203

Lucent Books
27500 Drake Rd.
Farmington Hills, MI 48331

ISBN-13: 978-1-4205-1243-4
ISBN-10: 1-4205-1243-9

Printed in the United States of America
2 3 4 5 6 7 19 18 17 16 15

TABLE OF CONTENTS

Many people today are amazed by the amount of nutrition and health information, often contradictory, that can be found in the media. Television, newspapers, and magazines bombard readers with the latest news and recommendations. Television news programs report on recent scientific studies. The healthy living sections of newspapers and magazines offer information and advice. In addition, electronic media such as websites, blogs, and forums post daily nutrition and health news and recommendations.

This constant stream of information can be confusing. The science behind nutrition and health is constantly evolving. Current research often leads to new ideas and insights. Many times, the latest nutrition studies and health recommendations contradict previous studies or traditional health advice. When the media reports these changes without giving context or explanations, consumers become confused. In a survey by the National Health Council, for example, 68 percent of participants agreed that "when reporting medical and health news, the media often contradict themselves, so I don't know what to believe." In addition, the Food Marketing Institute reported that eight out of ten consumers thought it was likely that nutrition and health experts would have a completely different idea about what foods are healthy within five years. With so much contradictory information, people have difficulty deciding how to apply nutrition and health recommendations to their lives. Students find it difficult to find relevant, yet clear and credible information for reports.

Changing recommendations for antioxidant supplements are an example of how confusion can arise. In the 1990s antioxidants such as vitamins C and E and beta-carotene came to the public's attention. Scientists found that people who ate more antioxidant-rich foods had a lower risk of heart disease, cancer, vision loss, and other chronic conditions than those who ate lower amounts. Without waiting for more scientific study, the media and supplement companies quickly spread the word that antioxidants could help fight and prevent disease. They recommended that people take antioxidant supplements and eat fortified foods. When further scientific studies were completed, however, most did not support the initial recommendations. While naturally occurring antioxidants in fruits and vegetables may help prevent a variety of chronic diseases, little scientific evidence proved antioxidant supplements had the same effect. In fact, a study published in the November 2008 *Journal of the American Medical Association* found that supplemental vitamins A and C gave no more heart protection than a placebo. The study's results contradicted the widely publicized recommendation, leading to consumer confusion. This example highlights the importance of context for evaluating nutrition and health news. Understanding a topic's scientific background, interpreting a study's findings, and evaluating news sources are critical skills that help reduce confusion.

Lucent's Nutrition and Health series is designed to help young people sift through the mountain of confusing facts, opinions, and recommendations. Each book contains the most recent up-to-date information, synthesized and written so that students can understand and think critically about nutrition and health issues. Each volume of the series provides a balanced overview of today's hot-button nutrition and health issues while presenting the latest scientific findings and a discussion of issues surrounding the topic. The series provides young people with tools for evaluating conflicting and ever-changing ideas about nutrition and health. Clear narrative peppered with personal anecdotes, fully documented primary and secondary source quotes, informative sidebars, fact boxes, and statistics are all used to help readers understand these topics and how they affect their bodies and their lives. Each volume includes information about changes in trends over time, political controversies, and international perspectives. Full-color photographs and charts enhance all volumes in the series. The Nutrition and Health series is a valuable resource for young people to understand current topics and make informed choices for themselves.

Farming Returns to the Old Ways

For most Americans, the word *farming* brings to mind fond images of barns and green fields with horses, cows, chickens, and pigs wandering among them. At grocery stores and supermarkets, shoppers may choose cartons of milk or boxes of cereal because those familiar barnyard images seem to promise wholesome goodness within. In reality, however, most modern farms are not nostalgic country enterprises, but rather massive corporations. Geometric rows of identical plants stretch as far as the eye can see. Airplanes buzz overhead, spraying clouds of chemicals to poison unwanted bugs and weeds. Giant machines rumble through fields to do the planting and the harvesting. Hundreds or even thousands of animals may live out their days in crowded pens.

Much of the food from these farms is shipped by truck to factories. There, machines peel, slice, or mash it, mix it with dyes and preservatives, and package it into Styrofoam trays, plastic bags, or cardboard boxes that are shipped in more trucks to stores across the country. A large percentage of the food Americans consume has been sprayed, infused, or mixed with chemicals they cannot even pronounce, much less define.

Throughout the past 150 years, farming has made a gradual but steady shift toward industrialization. A main goal has

Much of today's food is shipped long distances from farms to grocery stores using trucks.

been growing more food on less land and requiring less manual labor to do it. Food shoppers have been responsible for many of the changes by preferring, even demanding, foods that come in convenient, attractive, serving-sized packages that can sit in a cupboard for months without spoiling.

Starting in the early 1900s, some people began to have misgivings about these new, industrialized foods. By the 1960s, a growing number of North Americans, along with people in Europe and other parts of the world, began to call for a return to natural farming and food production. By 1990, so many Americans demanded it that the U.S. government passed the Organic Foods Production Act. Like similar laws in other countries, it created two food industries in the United States—one that produced food using modern inventions and methods and one that required farmers to follow more traditional and natural techniques. The latter, organic food, has become an industry of its own.

Organic foods have never sold as well as traditional ones. Yet they are steadily gaining in popularity as more and more people become wary not just of pesticides and other chemicals in their food, but of processes such as the genetic modification of plants and the use of hormones and antibiotics on animals. The organic food industry was worth $35 billion by 2014, becoming big business itself. Its momentum is driven by consumers' wishes to avoid dangerous foods and to help the environment.

Organic food is not a cure-all for the world, however. People often misunderstand what organic labels mean, falsely believing that organic food is vastly more nutritious, for example, or that it will lead to weight loss. Fear drives some shoppers to purchase organic foods. They may believe conventionally farmed products are poisonous, even though scientific studies have found no evidence that this is true. Organic foods also tend to cost more money, making them difficult for many people to afford.

Organic foods have also led to disagreements about the global future of farming. One out of every eight human beings in the world today is chronically underfed. The more costly and time-intensive organic farming methods might not produce enough to improve this statistic or to feed the growing human population in the years to come. There is

Organic foods are gaining popularity as people become more concerned about pesticides and other chemicals in their foods.

also evidence, however, that industrial agricultural methods are damaging the environment for all future farming. Arguments for and against organic foods have much to do with the challenges of nourishing the world while also preserving it.

Shoppers have important choices to make about their food, and most Americans choose organic products at least some of the time. Learning what organic food is can help everyone make smart nutritional choices based on facts instead of assumptions.

CHAPTER 1

Food for a Modern World

Human beings have developed the technology to do many things in the world. They can travel and communicate globally, heal themselves from most illnesses, and even control many aspects of their environment. Despite these advancements, a seemingly simple challenge remains one of the most important and complex concerns facing the human race today—obtaining enough food for everyone on the planet.

The first humans, like all other creatures on earth, faced challenges to survival. They had to protect themselves from predators, find shelter, and raise children. Being social, they formed communities, combining families into larger groups. The most important concern was finding things to eat, because without food, no living thing can survive.

Early humans were gatherers and scavengers. They survived on plant-based foods such as nuts and berries and on the carcasses of animals that had been hunted and killed by other predators. Humans learned to make and use helpful tools such as baskets so they could gather many fruits at one time and share them with each other. They also learned to make weapons such as knives, spears, and bows and arrows that made it possible for them to hunt for fresh meat. Even with the use of tools, food was not always easy to come by.

Most plants die or go dormant during certain seasons of the year, and animals do not always stay in one place. In response to changes in the food supply they depended on, early humans were nomads, wandering from place to place to follow herds of animals they hunted or to find plant food during different seasons.

The Onset of Agriculture

In time, people discovered they did not have to rely entirely on nature's whims to feed themselves. They found that plants grow well along the banks of rivers, which begin in mountains where snow gathers in the winter. When the snow melts in spring, river water flows downhill, bringing with it vitamin-rich soil. Rivers often rise over their banks in spring, leaving behind moist soil that is nutritious and fertile. Once humans realized this, they began to make permanent homes along rivers, where they planted the seeds of their favorite food plants and grew crops to

Early people discovered that food plants grew well along the banks of rivers, and farms and civilizations began to develop in these areas.

feed themselves. It was the beginning of human agriculture.

Raising their own crops allowed people to grow enough food to stockpile it. This way, they had something to eat during cool or dry seasons when food did not grow as well. However, cultivating large crops of food was time-consuming, and it was difficult to grow many different types of crops. Communities of humans began to specialize in growing certain crops to trade with other people, and the first civilizations developed. "The adoption of agriculture made possible new settled lifestyles and set mankind on the path to the modern world," says science and technology writer Tom Standage. "Food subsequently acted as a tool of social organization, helping to shape and structure the complex societies that emerged."[1]

As humans came to depend on agriculture, societies shifted from small families that provided food just for themselves to large communities where different people had different roles or jobs. Some people grew food. Others traveled to central marketplaces to sell and trade food products with other growers. Landowners hired, or sometimes forced, people to grow and harvest crops. For the first time in human history, people had access to a fairly steady supply of staple foods that made up a majority of their diet, typically grains such as wheat, corn, and rice. They had time to experiment with growing different or more specialized foods that were more productive or tasted better. "Desirable traits were selected and propagated by early farmers," says Standage. "Mankind changed plants, and those plants in turn transformed mankind."[2]

NUTRITION FACT

4,500 years

Number of years ago when the first known use of pesticides took place. The Sumerians of Mesopotamia treated plants with sulfur compounds to kill insects and mites.

Shipping Food Supplies

Early agrarian societies also began to raise animals for meat, giving them even more variety in their diet. People were eager to trade their new food products. However, communities were often spread across large areas. Traveling by land in animal-drawn carts or by river or sea in boats often took so long that people's carefully grown plants or meats spoiled along the way. To avoid this, they developed methods for preserving produce and meat products. Fruits, vegetables, and spices could be dried to make them last longer, and salt was added to meat to prevent it from spoiling. Salt was the first food preservative, and it helped people transport food products not just from one town to another, but between regions and eventually across oceans to new continents.

As centuries passed, local agricultural societies gave way to a global food-trade industry. In the 1800s and 1900s, the Industrial Revolution began in Europe and spread to the United States and elsewhere around the world. New technology forever changed the way people cultivated, harvested, preserved, and ate their food. The invention of motorized, gasoline-powered engines led to machines farmers could use to plow, plant, and reap their harvests, making it possible to produce huge crops. Many foods were no longer processed and packaged by hand but in factories that could split them into equal, convenient portions encased in colorfully printed bags and boxes.

Meanwhile, the discovery that food stays fresh longer when it is kept cold led to the invention of refrigeration units. Ice boxes were used at first, followed by mechanical refrigerators and freezers powered by electricity. Refrigerated containers in train cars and ships, and eventually trucks and airplanes, made it possible to transport frozen food products almost anywhere in the world.

The biggest changes happened in the latter part of the twentieth century. Around the world, but especially in developed and industrialized countries such as the United States, most people no longer shopped at neighborhood markets for fresh, locally grown, in-season products. Instead, they bought food at centralized supermarkets, where shelves were lined with thousands of mass-produced, factory-packaged products. Fresh produce and meat was usually grown some distance away and transported to these stores in vehicles. "Grocery chains became a permanent fixture," say nutrition and food experts Amy Bentley and Hi'ilei Hobart, "eventually swallowing the older-style grocery as well as contributing to the decline of specialty stores such as butchers, fresh fruit markets, and bakeries."[3] Few people in industrial societies—especially Europe and North America—grew their own food anymore. Instead, food was obtained at a supermarket.

The Changing Nature of Agriculture

There were many advantages to supermarket shopping. For one thing, people could sample exotic foods that did not grow well in their region of the world. People in colder northern climates, for example, were able to eat citrus fruits, such as oranges and pineapples, that grew in warm places, and people who lived inland could buy shellfish and other seafood that had never been available to them before. The revolution in manufacturing and packaging also standardized food. Breakfast cereals, crackers, cookies, and dairy products were just some of the things that became associated with particular brands and the appearance of their packaging. Shoppers across an entire region, country, or even beyond could find familiar brands and products at any supermarket.

As agriculture became industrialized, particular brands developed that shoppers across the country could recognize in any store in which they shopped.

Such major shifts to the food industry had drawbacks, however. Especially in the United States, farmers were focused on selling food to thousands or potentially millions of customers. They began to devote vast expanses of land for agriculture. Farm crops became far too large for people to tend to all the plants, and were vulnerable to pests. Animals, insects, weeds, and fungi such as mold could destroy an entire crop, causing shortages and financial hardship for the farm's owner and employees.

To combat such threats to crops, farmers began experimenting with various chemicals added to the soil or applied to growing plants to keep pests away. This practice soon became commonplace, even though some of the chemicals were later shown to be harmful to both people and the environment.

Other problems with the new mass-produced food industry came about in the factories. There, grains such as wheat and rice along with starchy vegetables such as potatoes and corn were used to make foods such as crackers and snack chips. Factories added salt, sugar, and fat to make foods tasty, dyes to make them colorful, packaging to make them convenient, and chemical preservatives to give them a longer shelf life—the amount of time a food can sit in a store or pantry without rotting or getting stale.

In factories, naturally grown foods were transformed into products that often hardly resembled their original form. "Images of amber waves of wheat, lush fruit, and happy farm animals beckon from packages, and ads tout 'natural goodness,'" says food industry writer Melanie Warner. "On the subject of what happens between the picturesque farms and the supermarket aisles, manufacturers are generally mum."[4] People who questioned the safety of the methods and chemicals used to make highly processed foods turned to the government for guidance and advice.

A History of Food Laws

Food production was a big business in the United States long before the first supermarket. Crops grow well in American soil. The warm and fertile eastern and western coasts provide an abundance of fruit and vegetable crops,

Irish Potato Famine

In Ireland in the 1840s, potatoes were a staple food crop. About half of the Irish population, especially those who were poor and lived in rural areas, depended almost entirely on this single food source. During the wet summer of 1845, a plant mold disease swept across potato crops in Europe, killing most of the potato plants it infected. When the potato blight reached Ireland, it destroyed a food most Irish people ate every day, causing famine—population-wide starvation. The Irish government was unprepared to handle such a crisis, and a million people died of hunger or disease. Another million, desperate for food, fled Ireland and moved to other countries, especially the United States.

The famine lasted until 1850, when weather conditions changed and the blight receded. Europeans could grow potato crops again. However, the event taught Ireland and the United States powerful lessons about what can happen if a staple crop is destroyed. Preventing such famine became a major focus of American farmers and agriculture scientists. To this day, the fear of food shortages and crop failure prompts many to treat their crops with chemical pesticides before mold, insects, or other problems can set in and destroy the plants that feed entire regions.

A memorial to the victims of the Irish potato famine is on a quay in Dublin, Ireland.

while the Great Plains in the central part of the country provide enough grains to feed not just the American population but millions of people overseas as well. With so many people depending on American food, the U.S. government has a long history of passing laws and regulations about how plant and animal products should be raised, processed, and shipped.

In 1862, President Abraham Lincoln established the Bureau of Agriculture, a small government agency whose goal was to increase the country's crop production and conduct research on farming. The bureau employed four scientists who oversaw the country's farms, searched for new plants or plant varieties, and sought ways to improve growing methods. In 1867, the bureau was transformed into the U.S. Department of Agriculture (USDA). Its goals were mostly economic. Agricultural products had become an important export for the United States. By the turn of the twentieth century, the USDA employed about 2,500 people who worked to maximize the production of food crops that could feed Americans and also be shipped and sold outside the country.

In 1862, farmers had made up 58 percent of the American workforce, but by the end of the nineteenth century, that number had dropped to 43 percent. Smaller farms had once grown a variety of produce and raised different kinds of animals, but by the late 1800s, they began to convert to massive tracts of land that produced only one or two major crops or that specialized in raising a particular type of animal. These larger farms were tightly regulated by the government, whose main goal was maximizing how much food could be produced and sold. "Like any other sector of an industrial economy, agriculture must be organized according to principals of efficiency," says Paul B. Thompson, a professor of agriculture, food, and community ethics. "Agricultural policy specialists . . . would press forward with a new organization of American agriculture along the lines of the industrial model."[5] American farming and food production became a national business—and a big one.

Food Safety

Along with making discoveries about varieties of plants that yielded large crops, scientists were learning other things, too. Food produced and shipped in such huge amounts had the potential to make a lot of people sick if it contained anything harmful. By the early 1900s, the USDA's focus expanded from increasing the profits of the

French scientist Louis Pasteur developed the process called pasteurization that kills harmful bacteria in foods and drinks.

food industry to also ensuring that the food supply was safe for people to eat.

In 1856, a French scientist named Louis Pasteur discovered that briefly exposing liquids to very high heat killed harmful bacteria and helped prevent the liquids from spoiling. This process became known as pasteurization. In the early 1900s, the USDA mandated that all American-produced milk and dairy products be pasteurized before being sold to consumers. It was one of the points of the Pure Food and Drug Act of 1907, which established a system for government officials to inspect the safety of meat, dairy, and other food products sold in the United States.

New safety regulations such as pasteurization, along with industrial farming and food packaging methods, led to an even bigger boom in agricultural production. By the early decades of the 1900s, one farm tractor could do the work of seventeen men and fifty horses. Food was profitable and easy to grow. Wild grasses had once grown throughout the Midwest, feeding herds of grazing buffalo, but in the early 1900s, vast farms sprang up there as people used tractors to plow up the grassland and cultivate miles and miles of the rich, dark topsoil with big-money crops such as wheat. It seemed like the American food industry, now safe and government regulated, could never fail.

Then disaster struck. In 1931, it did not rain as expected. Rain did not come the next year, either. For the next decade, a drought—a prolonged lack of water—plagued the Great Plains. Topsoil that had once been held in place by native wild grasses blew away, filling the air with clouds of dirt in what became known as the Dust Bowl. The catastrophe lasted almost a decade. Throughout the 1930s, there was a severe drop in American food production and the money that came with it.

It was a powerful lesson for the American farm industry. In 1935, the government established the Soil Conservation Service to help battle the effects of the Dust Bowl and prevent a similar disaster from happening again. One change was a requirement to terrace sloped land, forming it into flat steps to keep water from draining downhill and carrying topsoil with it. Farmers also began to leave the previous year's crops in place at the end of each growing season so that the roots would hold soil down during winter winds. "The recurring dust storms and rivers yellow with silt are a warning that Nature's resources will not indefinitely withstand exploitation or negligence," President Franklin D. Roosevelt said in a 1936 speech. "The only permanent protection which can be given consumers must come from conservation practiced by farmers."[6]

War Resurrects Agriculture

Farms in the Great Plains recovered from the Dust Bowl by the end of the 1930s, but more changes were to come

Writers Tackle Agriculture

Vast changes to the American food production industry in the 1900s meant that for the first time in history, food was sold in places far away from where it was produced. Shoppers were largely oblivious to the methods used to get convenient food products from farms to stores, but some writers aimed to change that by publishing books that exposed shocking realities in American farming. In 1906, Upton Sinclair's *The Jungle* described the filthy, diseased conditions of slaughterhouses and factories where meat was packaged for American consumers. In 1939, John Steinbeck wrote *The Grapes of Wrath*, a novel about the desperation of migrant farm workers during the Dust Bowl of the 1930s and the selfishness of large landowners who cared more about money than people. In 1962, Rachel Carson's *Silent Spring* warned about the effects of agricultural poisons on the environment and specifically exposed the insecticide DDT, which weakens the shells of bird eggs so the baby birds cannot survive. All three books were very controversial, but they transformed Americans' views of conventional agriculture. These authors inspired people to support and seek out food that was grown and raised naturally instead of industrially, contributing to the development of modern standards for organic farming.

Upton Sinclair's book The Jungle *exposed the filthy and diseased conditions of meat packaging plants.*

to American farming. The United States needed both food and money when it entered World War II in 1941. During the war years, agricultural production was more important to the American economy than ever. The United States made money for its military resources by shipping food crops overseas to war-afflicted countries such as Great Britain and France, where food was scarce. Many of the United States' working-age men were fighting overseas, so efficient farming methods became more important than ever before. There was a sharp rise in the use of chemical fertilizers, substances that make soil more fertile, so that larger crops could be grown faster on less land. Farmers also sprayed more pesticides on their food crops to head off insects, weeds, and other damaging species.

When World War II ended in 1945 and soldiers returned home, American farming methods did not go back to the way things were before the war. Instead, between 1950 and 1970, agriculture in the United States became even more competitive and focused on efficiency. The total amount of land used for farming decreased, as did the amount of time people spent working the land, but farm productivity surged by 50 percent. The invention of new and improved farming tools and machines made this surge in farm productivity possible, and an increasing demand for food in a world with a rapidly growing population made it desirable and profitable to grow more crops than ever before. "In no other period in history were the agricultural gains quite so dramatic as they were from 1950 to 1970," says history professor Paul K. Conkin. "Change was so rapid that almost no one was able to measure, or comprehend, what was happening."[7] The use of chemical fertilizers and pesticides quadrupled during this period to help meet the demand for more food grown in less time and on less land. This led to renewed questions about whether these products were safe for people or the environment.

The Call for Chemical Cutbacks

As natural methods of growing crops and raising poultry and livestock were increasingly replaced by industrial ones, most people accepted the new innovations just as they accepted other technological marvels, such as automobiles, television, and telephones. Not everyone was pleased with the changes, however. In the 1940s and 1950s, some farmers around the country had already started to turn away from

California Certified Organic Farmers

Certified Grower

Organically grown in accordance with the California Organic Foods Act of 199[?]

farming techniques that relied on chemicals and industrial machinery, preferring to grow food in ways that worked with nature rather than battled it. Some of these small farmers banded together in states such as Texas and California to establish small markets and sell their own food. In the 1970s, a group called California Certified Organic Farmers became the first organization to define goals for growing food naturally. They created the first set of standards for farmers to follow in order to label the food they produced as "organic."

Throughout the 1970s and 1980s, the organic foods movement gained strength as more studies showed that agricultural chemicals were affecting the environment, plant and animal populations, and human health. In 1990, the U.S. Congress passed the Organic Foods Production Act, which in turn led to the creation of the National Organic Standards—a set of rules and regulations farmers had to follow if they were to label their food as organic. The rules specified, among other things, that organic foods had to be produced and handled without the use of certain chemicals.

The California Certified Organic Farmers became the first organization to outline goals for growing food organically.

The demand for and availability of organic foods has grown dramatically in the years since. As of 2014, three out of four American grocery stores and supermarkets sold organic foods, and about 4 percent of all food sold in the United States was labeled organic. Fresh produce is the most popular category of organic food, but American consumers increasingly buy organic versions of meat and dairy products, breads and grains, packaged and processed foods, and even condiments such as ketchup. "The explosive growth in market share for organic produce in recent years testifies to a simple fact that pesticide companies and the farmers who use their products just can't seem to grasp: people don't like to eat food contaminated by pesticides,"[8] says Ken Cook, president and co-founder of the Environmental Working Group, an organization that supports organic foods.

Despite the surge in demand for organic products, however, there is some confusion over what organic food is and is not. People also disagree on the effects organic production and consumption might have on people, the environment, and the economy. Organic products have become a controversial issue in the United States, and there is high demand for correct and updated information about this growing trend in food.

CHAPTER 2

Organic Food and People's Health

Many chemicals used in modern industrial agriculture have the potential to cause major health problems such as poisoning. Some studies suggest they might also lead to diseases such as cancer and autism, a mental condition that appears in early childhood and causes difficulty with language, communication, and socializing. To date, the people most affected by exposure to agriculture-related chemicals have been those who work on farms or live close to them, but there are ongoing scientific studies to determine whether eating foods treated with various chemicals can affect people's health. "As with any technology, the use of such chemicals [is] not without certain risks," says food safety consultant Gerald G. Moy. "These need to be addressed and actively managed."[9] The growing popularity of organic foods, which are intended to be grown or raised with few or no chemicals, is largely an effect of widespread uneasiness about the potential dangers of applying unnatural things to natural products.

The Purpose of Pesticides

A big concern about the safety of plant foods is the amount of pesticides to which they are exposed. The word *pesticide*

Spraying pesticides on crops ensures the crops remain free of plant-killing insects, rodents, weeds, and other pests. Pesticides also may contaminate food with poisonous residues.

comes from the Latin root *–cide*, which means "killer" or "the act of killing." Pesticides are poisons for agricultural pests, organisms that damage the plants a farmer is trying to grow. Pests can be animals like rodents, plants like weeds, insects like caterpillars and aphids, fungi like mold, or even bacteria. Different types of organisms afflict different crops, and this has led to the classifications of pesticides. Herbicides, for example, kill invading plants and insecticides kill insects. Even within these classifications there is variation. One insecticide may target aphids that feed on grape plants, while another may kill earworms, which are moth larvae that feed on ears of corn.

Pests have always plagued farmers. At the very least, they are a costly nuisance. "To ensure adequate food production, it is necessary to control weeds, fungal pathogens, and insects, each of which poses a threat of yield-losses of about 13–15% before harvest,"[10] say agricultural researchers Mark Drewes, Klaus Tietjen, and Thomas C. Sparks. Pests also have the potential to ruin entire crops, however. This can be disappointing for someone who gardens as a hobby, but for a family or business depending on food crops as its source of income, it can be devastating. Invasive pests can even destroy the food an entire community, cultural group, or country depends on, leaving them with little or nothing to eat.

NUTRITION FACT

California has more than twice as many certified organic farms as any other U.S. state.

In industrial societies like the United States, widespread crop destruction usually does not lead to widespread starvation, but it could mean that popular foods such as oranges and avocados are unavailable or become so rare that they are very expensive. It can also take a long time for slow-growing plants, such as fruit trees, to recover from pest damage.

Pesticide use increases farm productivity by reducing or eliminating the destruction of plants by many kinds of unwanted invaders. However, many people are concerned about the potential effects these chemical poisons might have on people who ingest them. "Despite the benefits of pesticide usages, they can cause injury to human health as well as the environment," says Sameeh Mansour, a professor of pesticides and environmental toxicology. "Pesticides move through air, soil, and water and find their way . . . through the food chain, eventually to enter the human diet."[11] When chemicals are applied to plants like fruits and vegetables, people might consume them directly. So do the animals that feed on pesticide-treated plants, such as chickens that eat treated corn or cattle that eat treated hay. People who then consume meat from these animals might also be ingesting chemicals that have built up in the animals' bodies.

Despite people's growing concern over pesticide use on human food, consumers themselves have a role in driving the increased use of agricultural pesticides. For example, shoppers usually shun foods such as corn and apples that have worms in them, even though the worms are not known to make people sick. Most customers pick through piles of produce looking for fruits and vegetables with no visible pest damage. "They [produce shoppers] pick up a tomato, put it

Pest Predators

Farming and gardening creates a habitat for many uninvited insect invaders. Organic growing methods scorn or outright forbid most chemical pesticides, but farmers can outsmart troubling insects with the help of other critters. Ladybugs and butterflies can be great assets to an organic garden because they eat pests like aphids. Wasps and yellow jackets are effective killers of plant pests like cabbageworms. Ducks and chickens feast on many kinds of beetles, worms, and insect larvae, as do wild birds like robins, bluebirds, and sparrows. Organic farmers even welcome creepier critters like spiders, bats, and garter snakes, all of which munch on bugs.

Farmers who recruit these garden warriors hope to ward off plant damage without resorting to poisons. The key is to identify which natural predators to pair with troubling insects and then create a welcoming habitat for them. Farmers can plant certain types of wildflowers near and among their crops to draw in butterflies, or they can plant trees to encourage robins and sparrows to make homes. Wasps can be enticed with floorless birdhouses, where they like to build nests. Organic farmers can spare themselves much work and worry by inviting natural predators to pitch in.

Some organic farmers choose to use natural predators—such as this ladybug which eats aphids—instead of pesticides to protect their crops.

back down, walk away," says produce marketing consultant Ron Pelger. "And they'll tell me: 'Oh there was a spot on it, it's bad.' That tomato would taste fine, but it doesn't change the situation."[12] By showing a strong preference for pest-free products, consumers give farmers a strong incentive to use pesticides so that their produce sells well in stores.

On Fertile Ground

Fertilizers are another chemical concern many people have about modern farming methods. Farming is a seasonal activity, meaning most plants grow naturally during certain seasons and die off during others. There are ideal times to plant and harvest certain crops, but if farmers can grow and harvest two plant crops in a season instead of just one, they can double their profits. The farming industry always seeks new ways to grow more plants in less time.

Boosting crop productivity does not always happen entirely naturally. All plants need water, air, and sunlight to survive, but to be healthy, they also absorb nutrients from the soil they grow in. When the plants die, their bodies decompose and return nutrients to the soil for the next season's plants to use. When plants are harvested instead of being left to decompose, however, fewer nutrients return to the soil. In time, especially if more than one crop is grown on an area of land during a single season, the soil becomes depleted of nutrients. If that happens, future generations of plants may be scrawny or unable to grow at all.

Restoring vital nutrients to the soil before planting new crops results in larger, healthier plants and can even ensure that they produce more fruits and vegetables. Three of the most important plant nutrients are nitrogen, phosphorous, and potassium, a trio known as N-P-K because of their chemical symbols. Manure, or the droppings of large animals like horses and cattle, contains these nutrients and has been a common fertilizer for centuries, but modern farmers also use man-made, chemical fertilizers. These are often granular, in the form of easy-to-spread grains, and they contain enough N-P-K to quickly and easily replace what is lost in the soil during a growing season. "Increases in worldwide food production demands are creating the need for new solutions in the agriculture industry," says Anna Neumeier, a marketing specialist for the fertilizer manufacturing company FEECO International. "Applying the proper inputs [such as granular fertilizers] in the right place, at the right time, in the appropriate amounts will achieve optimal yield for the entire field."[13]

Chemical fertilizers are not without drawbacks, however. For one thing, nitrogen, phosphorous, and potassium must be bound to other chemicals, often heavy metals such as zinc and lead, to turn them into a solid form that can be added to soil. The unused N-P-K and other elements remain in the soil, and as more fertilizer is added from season to season, these chemicals build up.

Over time, there may be so many surplus elements in the soil that the plants begin to absorb them. In turn, people who consume the plants also ingest these chemicals, which can cause health problems if they build up in the body. People have become concerned about eating produce grown in soil that is treated with chemical fertilizers. "Heavy metals become toxic when they do not get metabolized by the body and end up accumulating in the soft tissues," says crop and soil scientist Sam Angima. Instead of being digested and moving out of the body, traces of metals can accumulate, especially in fatty tissues. It is rare for heavy metals to build up to amounts that are dangerous to people's health, but if it happens, the metals can cause a number of serious problems, such as gastrointestinal trouble and interference with brain function and development. Many people are therefore concerned about the possibility of eating heavy metals in fertilizer-treated produce. "Since most of the ingestion of

Like this farmer, organic farmers may choose to fertilize their crops with organic material such as manure.

heavy metals occurs from [the] consumption of plants, then addressing how plants acquire heavy metals can aid in controlling heavy metal toxicity,"[14] says Angima.

Organic food growers try to avoid the need for synthetic fertilizers that contain heavy metals. One way to do this is by rotating crops, which means growing different types of plants from season to season. Different plants use nutrients in different amounts, and some even help restore nutrients such as nitrogen to the soil, so crop rotation helps prevent the soil from being depleted of essential nutrients as quickly. Organic farmers also try to let certain fields lie dormant, or unplanted, every few seasons to let the soil rest.

If organic growers do fertilize soil, they may choose natural fertilizers such as compost—decayed organic material that is rich in the nutrients plants need but which does not include harmful chemicals. Many people consider this return to an old method of fertilizing to be a positive step toward improved agriculture. "A century ago," says food and agriculture expert Dan Charles, "synthetic fertilizer seemed like an easy shortcut out of scarcity. . . . This time the innovations that save us—and our planet—may not be invented in a chemistry laboratory. Instead they may come from farmers and fields in every corner of the world."[15]

Boosting Growth with Hormones

Another thing many farmers do to increase the productivity of their crops is apply hormones to the plants. Hormones are chemical messengers produced naturally in both plants and animals. They are carried, through a plant's sap or an animal's blood or body fluids, to specific parts of the body where they act as triggers to make cells do or stop doing certain things. Hormones are essential to life because they help regulate processes such as growth, reproduction, and death. In plants, for example, hormones do things such as telling stems and branches to grow longer.

Two plant hormones that are important to farmers are gibberellin and ethylene. The gibberellin hormone has many functions in plants, but one of the most critical is that it tells seeds when it is time to germinate, or sprout. Most plants' seeds have a dormant phase in which they are alive but not growing. They wait for the right time of year to give the tiny, tender new seedlings the best chance for survival. During the cold winter, for example, an absence of gibberellin tells seeds to lie dormant for several more months, awaiting the warmer season.

If farmers expose seeds to man-made chemicals that mimic gibberellin, however, the seeds can be tricked into sprouting any time. As long as farmers ensure that the newly sprouted seedlings have the right temperature and the correct amounts of light and water, such as by putting them in a greenhouse, new crops can be started all year. People no longer have to wait for seeds to grow in natural yearly cycles.

Ethylene is another hormone related to plant growth. Instead of affecting the seeds, it works by telling fruit-producing plants when their fruit should begin to ripen. Ripening tends to happen rapidly across a crop because ethylene is airborne, meaning it can travel as a gas through the air. When some plants start producing ethylene, the fruit of neighboring plants also starts to ripen. Farmers must then scramble to harvest the fruit, because once fruit ripens, it usually begins to decompose within a few days. Controlling the chemical ripening signal can help farmers delay or slow down the ripening process, giving them more time to harvest their fruit and transport it to stores. The ripening process can even be timed so that consumers buy fruit and vegetables just as they reach ripeness.

Farmers use hormones for other reasons, as well. Hormones make plants grow faster and produce fruit sooner, and they can also make some fruits and vegetables grow larger. Hormones are even used to control invasive and unwanted plants. When applied to a field of crops that has been infested with weeds, certain hormones will target just the weeds' growing cycle so that they die without affecting the desired plants.

The use of plant hormones in agriculture has many benefits, but it is not without controversy. Synthetic plant growth regulators (PGRs), applied to plants to coax them out of their natural behavior patterns, have been used since the 1930s. The Environmental Protection Agency (EPA), the agency

The hormone ethylene works by encouraging the ripening process in fruit-producing plants such as strawberries.

of the U.S. government that protects human health and the environment, regulates PGRs and determines the quantities in which farmers can use them. Some PGRs have been banned because when tested they were found to have possible damaging effects on animals that consume the treated plants. Other PGRs have yet to be tested, so their effects are unknown. "From the regulatory control perspective, plant growth regulators are classified under 'pesticides,'"[16] says food safety expert Joan Yau.

NUTRITION FACT

Coffee

The most abundant and most profitable organic product imported into the U.S.

Not all PGRs are necessarily harmful, but the organic food industry is cautious about the use of any synthetic hormones on plants. By growing smaller crops and selling them at local markets close to their farms, many organic farmers have no need to delay the ripening of fruit or vegetables. "When grown locally, the crops are picked at their peak of ripeness versus being harvested early in order to be shipped and distributed to your local retail store,"[17] says Rita Klavinski, a health and food safety educator for Michigan State University Extension. Selling to customers in their own community is one of the ways organic farmers can avoid the hormones some larger growers depend on.

Growing Beefier Animals

Hormones are also very important to the development of animals, including those that make up a significant portion of the agriculture industry. Many farmers raise poultry (such as chickens and turkeys) and livestock (primarily cattle, hogs, and sheep) and sell the meat, eggs, and dairy products. Cattle and sheep are the only animals for which the U.S. government has legalized hormone use, but livestock hormones are nevertheless very controversial.

Animal hormones do much the same thing as plant hormones do—they are chemical messengers that travel through the body and tell the animal when to grow, mature, and reproduce. Growth hormones, therefore, can increase the size, growth rate, and overall productivity of animals. This issue has received much attention by scientists, nutritionists, and the media.

The American cattle industry, which produces most of the meat and dairy products consumed in the United States, has used hormones since the 1950s. Animals are given a boost of naturally occurring hormones that stimulate development, growth, and reproduction. Typically, pellets of the hormones are placed in incisions, or shallow cuts, on the backside of the animals' ears, where they dissolve and enter the bloodstream. The hormone boost makes the animals grow and mature more quickly. Hormones also improve an animal's ability to convert the plant material it eats into lean meat.

Beef hormones have been a source of much controversy, and many people express concerns over whether consuming hormone-treated beef may lead to negative health effects in humans. However, according to the U.S. Meat Export Federation (USMEF), a nonprofit organization that has studied meat safety in the United States for three decades, the level of hormones remaining in beef sold to consumers is far too small to affect health. "A three-ounce serving of beef from an animal treated with natural estradiol contains 1.9 nanograms of [the hormone] estrogen," says the USMEF. "This compares to 1.2 nanograms in an untreated animal. A difference of seven-tenths of a billionth of a gram is indeed trivial when compared to the 136,000 nanograms produced every day in a man's body, and 480,000 produced in a woman's body." Furthermore, the USMEF says, vegetables naturally have hormones, too, and in far greater amounts than beef: "A standard serving of potatoes, for instance, contains 225 nanograms of estrogen, compared to beef's 1.9 nanograms."[18]

Female dairy cows are treated with a different hormone than bulls, which are males used for breeding, or steers, which are males slaughtered for meat. Cows are injected with bovine growth hormone, or bGH (*bovine* means relating to cows or cattle). This hormone, approved by the U.S. Food and Drug Administration (FDA) in 1993 for use in dairy cattle, stimulates them to produce as much as 20 percent more milk. Numerous studies conducted by many unrelated scientific and health-regulation organizations have found no link between disease, ill health, or other unintended effects in humans and the use of hormones in American-raised cattle or sheep (the only other animals that can legally be given hormones in the United States).

Many consumers, however, still have concerns about the use of hormones in livestock. Injecting or imbedding hormones into animals is not a natural process, and therefore, the organic food industry considers hormone-treated beef, lamb, and dairy products as straying from its ultimate goal of

Bacteria can devastate an entire crop, as happened to this onion crop in Thailand.

who ingest these microscopic organisms can suffer from severe vomiting, diarrhea, and even kidney failure. Non-organic produce may contain harmful bacteria as well, but consumers potentially face a higher risk of such illness when they purchase organic food that has not been treated with antibiotics.

Widespread antibiotic use can also be dangerous, however, because bacteria are able to change and adapt rapidly. Some strains of bacteria have become resistant to antibiotics, meaning that the drugs used to kill them are no longer effective. Antibiotic-resistant bacteria are a public health problem because people can become infected with some of these bacteria. Such an infection can be deadly if the drugs that have traditionally been used to treat it are no longer effective. "There is no doubt that with billions of animals being treated with antibiotics in our country, . . . that there are many more 'factories' of antibiotic resistant organisms among the animals,"[20] says molecular biologist Stuart B. Levy, president of the Alliance for the Prudent Use of Antibiotics.

Whether chemicals come in the form of fertilizers, pesticides, hormones, or antibiotics, supporters of organic foods want to see less of them in the food supply—or even none at all. Organic food supporters, concerned about potential and as-yet-unknown health effects of such chemicals in the food and liquids people consume, are strongly opposed to their use and demand chemical-free food options, which they believe to be safer.

Organic Food and the Environment

Human health is not the only thing that concerns supporters of organic food. They also worry about the strain the rapidly growing human population—and the pressures of feeding it—are putting on the environment. The human race has existed for tens of thousands of years, but the worldwide population did not reach 1 billion people until about A.D. 1800. Since then, it has taken only slightly more than two hundred years for that population to grow by another 6 billion. As of 2013, there were 7.2 billion people living on earth, and the population currently grows by about 80 million people per year, approximately equal to the number of people who live in Germany.

This rapid growth of the human race puts a burden on the planet. Simply providing places for so many people to live and ways to cope with their waste products has become a daunting task. Providing energy to light people's homes and businesses and making sure they have transportation is another concern. One of the most pressing issues about the increasing human population, however, is making sure everyone has enough to eat. Growing food for billions of people has become one of the greatest of all human challenges, and it affects the planet in many major ways.

CHAPTER 3

Global Poisons

DDT is a powerful pesticide that was developed in 1939 and was first widely used during World War II to kill insects that carried diseases like malaria and yellow fever. Following the war, farmers in the United States began using DDT to control insects on plant crops. In the early 1970s, however, DDT was identified as harmful to people, wildlife, and the environment and was banned in the United States by the Environmental Protection Agency (EPA). It has since been banned by many other countries, and in 2004, it was among the twelve most toxic man-made substances named by the Stockholm Convention on Persistent Organic Pollutants. These toxins share certain characteristics: They do not break down quickly into less harmful forms and therefore persist in the environment for years or even decades; they accumulate in the fatty tissue of animals and people who consume them; and they can drift because they evaporate and become airborne. Many countries prohibit the use of poisons on this list, but chemicals drifting in the air pay no heed to national boundaries.

A worldwide ban of these substances seems essential, but enforcing such a ban could come at a dreadful cost. DDT, for example, is still used in Africa, South America, and Asia to help control mosquitoes that carry malaria, an often deadly disease that sickens 500 million people every year. Without DDT, malaria would infect millions more. Until effective alternatives are found, harmful pesticides like DDT may be a necessity.

Certain climates and land formations, such as deserts, the icy North and South Poles, and rugged mountain ranges, are not places where people can easily live or raise food. Much of the earth's inhabitable land is currently used for planting crops and raising animals for food. As the world's population continues to grow, more and more agricultural land will be needed. However, modern farming methods, especially those that developed during and since the early twentieth century, have already led to the destruction of much of the world's farmable land, making it unsuitable for future food production. When this happens, food growers must find new places to grow crops and raise animals. Many modern farming methods also cause pollution and waste limited natural resources.

Agricultural practices of large-scale industrial farms were developed to feed a lot of people quickly, and for decades, they seemed to work well. However, as time goes on, many of these practices are proving impossible to maintain. "We are going to see significant changes in the way we involve ourselves with food if we continue to take out the earth's limited resources at this unsustainable rate,"[21] says agriculture expert Fred Kirschenmann. Many of the principles of the organic food industry are an attempt to change the widespread, negative effects of industrial agriculture so that the earth and its resources can be preserved for future generations.

Pollution by Fossil Fuels

Since the invention of engines powered by gasoline or diesel fuel in the early 1900s, much of the work of farming has been accomplished by tractors and other large machines. Once plant crops are grown and harvested, the produce is usually carried away from the farm by trucks, trains, or airplanes. Some produce goes directly to stores and supermarkets. Many other harvested products such as grain, corn, and potatoes are shipped to factories and made into foods such as flour, pasta, breakfast cereal, and potato chips. Meat and dairy products from livestock and poultry farms are also processed at large industrial centers. Factories require a lot of electrical power, which in most urban areas is provided partly or mostly by burning coal or natural gas. The products manufactured at food processing plants are then shipped once more, typically by truck, train, or plane, to reach consumers via grocery stores and supermarkets all over the country and often around the world.

According to the University of Michigan's Center for Sustainable Systems, every ton of food produced on a farm in

the United States and shipped to consumers ultimately uses seven times that amount of fossil fuels. Food production contributes significantly to air pollution while also depleting limited natural resources. "Industrialized agriculture requires large inputs of fossil fuels," says public health specialist Steve Wing, and "large transportation corridors for agricultural products lead to excess air pollution from ports, rail terminals, [and] road traffic."[22]

Many organic farmers try to minimize the amount of fossil fuels they use and release into the environment by operating smaller farms and doing as much work as possible by hand to reduce their reliance on gasoline- or diesel-fueled machines. Some organic farmers have even returned to using plow animals such as horses and mules to help them work the soil and plant crops. One of the most significant ways many organic farmers reduce their dependence on fossil fuels, though, is by selling their food to people and markets located nearby, rather than shipping it to distant processing plants and supermarkets. Preserving the environment

The factories in which most food is processed require the use of large amounts of fossil fuels, which leads to pollution of the atmosphere.

and its resources with steps like these is a main goal of the organic food movement.

Pollution by Pesticides

The polluting by-products of farm tractors and factories are not the only source of contamination caused by agriculture. Chemical pesticides also have damaging effects on the environment. Some of these toxic agricultural chemicals mix with the air, potentially making people sick if they inhale them. "When pesticides are applied to agricultural fields, their vapors may drift, exposing both workers and nearby community residents,"[23] say health science experts Robert Friis and Thomas Sellers. A practice called crop dusting, which involves using airplanes to spray whole fields of plants with pesticides, adds considerably to air pollution.

Organic farmers are committed to lessening or completely avoiding toxic chemicals, often using natural methods instead for controlling pests. For example, they may plant a variety of crops in an area, including plants that insects prefer over the crops farmers want to grow. Weed control, too, can often be accomplished without toxic chemicals. Simply rotating, or regularly changing, the types of crops grown on an area of land can help, because some weeds grow better among some crops than others. Changing crops often prevents any single weed species from dominating the area season after season. Farmers can also plant cover crops, which directly compete with weeds and keep them from sprouting and seeding. To control certain molds and other types of fungi, farmers may simply need to space out crops and angle rows of plants to take advantage of the wind. Improved airflow and leaving distance between plants can be very effective at preventing mold.

Such practices require farmers to study and experiment with natural biological processes instead of chemicals, but organic farmers believe such methods may be adequate to successfully protect and nourish crops. "Rather than

NUTRITION FACT

5.4 gallons (20L)

Amount of water it takes to grow a single head of broccoli.

Agricultural irrigation often leads to runoff, in which excess fertilizer and pesticides may end up in rivers, lakes, and oceans.

go in there and spray a bunch of stuff on it, we let nature do its thing,"[24] says Randy Hoovey, an organic farmer in Illinois.

Pollution by Fertilizers

Burned fossil fuels and widespread pesticides are drawbacks of conventional farming, but chemical fertilizers do their own damage to the environment. These fertilizers are mixed into the soil, but the crop plants usually do not use all of the extra nutrients. Farmers regularly irrigate their crops, providing water to them usually with sprinklers or by flooding fields to moisten the soil. These methods cause runoff, excess water that the topsoil cannot absorb. Runoff sinks into water stores deep below the ground's surface, known as groundwater, or trickles downhill and collects into streams. Runoff water from agricultural fields ultimately finds its way into rivers, lakes, and oceans, often carrying with it traces of pesticides and fertilizers.

Excess nutrients left over from fertilized farmland are especially problematic when they enter water sources. If surpluses of nutrients such as nitrogen, phosphorous, and potassium flood rivers and lakes, they can directly poison natural plant and animal species, but they also cause an increase in the growth of water organisms such as algae, which feast on the extra nutrients fertilizers provide. Algae can use up all the oxygen in the water, disrupting the delicate balance of wildlife in rivers and lakes and potentially killing any fish and other species that live there. In addition, as fertilizers and other chemicals seep into sources of drinking water, humans and animals may have no choice but to consume them.

The use of fertilizers in farming has already polluted many of the earth's freshwater sources. In the United States alone, "Agricultural activities impair more [U.S.] streams than any other class of human impacts: approximately 40% of stream miles and 16% of lakes and reservoirs," says climate policy specialist Elisa Lanzi. "The overgrown, turbid, oxygen-starved, and sometimes smelly water bodies are less appealing to human recreators and residents, just as they are to aquatic organisms that require clearer waters."[25]

Wasted Water

Not only does industrial agriculture infuse water with chemicals, it also wastes huge volumes of it. The earth is covered with so much water that it seems impossible for mankind to use it all. However, the vast majority of water is found in salty oceans. Just 3 percent of the planet's water is fresh. People, plants, and animals all depend on this tiny fraction of the planet's liquid for their survival, and humans have developed ways to draw it from rivers, streams, and lakes or pump it from deep underground. The majority of all freshwater collected by these methods is used to water food crops. As more and more people require ever bigger crops for food, freshwater supplies are being strained, and that poses many serious concerns not just for people but for all life on earth.

"We're going deeper into debt on our groundwater use, and that has very significant impacts for global water security," says Sandra Postel, director of the Global Water Policy Project. "The rate of groundwater depletion has doubled since 1960."[26] Adding to the problem, as much as 60 percent of the freshwater used in agriculture is wasted by inefficient irrigation methods. Sprinklers that are used to water large fields of crops spray water into the air, for example, where much of it evaporates, changing into water vapor before it can reach the soil below.

Crops that are instead irrigated by flooding methods do not cause as much water to be lost by evaporation, but chemical salts, a common ingredient in fertilizers, accumulate in the water as it seeps through the soil. Like excess nitrogen, salt collected in farm runoff water is carried into streams, lakes, and groundwater, raising the salinity, or salt content, of these freshwater sources. On a planet covered with salty water, agriculture is making even more saltwater out of the very limited freshwater sources that all land animals and plants depend on for life.

Still another problem is water that seeps through the soil where poultry or livestock are raised. This water collects bacteria and parasites from animal waste on its way to rivers, streams, and lakes, potentially infecting these water sources with unwanted organisms. Water can be treated to remove harmful bacteria or parasites, but this process is costly. Wastewater treatment is an unreachable goal for some developing countries, such as Indonesia in Southeast Asia and Tanzania in Africa. In these and other parts of the world, runoff water containing agricultural and even human waste products is simply reused by being pulled out of polluted rivers and lakes to irrigate more crops. Harmful bacteria and parasites infect not just drinking water, but the entire food supply where this happens.

Death Downstream

The Gulf of Mexico is home to many oceanic plants and animals, but it is also the location of a huge dead zone—an area of ocean where there is not enough oxygen for most things to live. Agricultural chemicals that collect from farms along the Mississippi River ultimately get dumped into the Gulf to cause this yearly dead zone, which averages about 5,000 square miles (13,000km²), roughly the size of Connecticut. Algae feast on the nutrients in chemical fertilizers and reproduce quickly, using up the oxygen other species need. Animals like fish and shrimp can move to better habitats, but plants cannot. As water plants die each year, so do many animal species, vastly reducing diversity in what was once a thriving ocean habitat.

The Gulf's dead zone is one of more than 550 similar man-made dead zones and is the second largest in the world, smaller only than a zone in the Baltic Sea. Dead zones are not permanent, and since 1972, scientists have been studying ways to shrink the Gulf's dead zone so the ocean can recover. The solutions, however, include major changes to industrial farming methods upriver. Such changes are difficult and slow to implement.

This image shows the Mississippi River emptying into the Gulf of Mexico.

Irrigating food crops with untreated wastewater sickens or kills millions of people worldwide every year, and illnesses are not just limited to underdeveloped countries. Many crops, such as cocoa and coffee beans, are exported from underdeveloped countries to other parts of the world, including the United States. Plants grown with untreated wastewater, therefore, could potentially affect people living in developed countries even though they have better water treatment practices, although this happens very rarely and is not considered a serious food concern in the United States.

Farms That Help

With freshwater in short supply, conserving and caring for the planet's water sources is a critical issue for food growers. Organic farmers, especially, seek irrigation methods that require less water and also waste less of it. Organic farms in places that are frequently drought-stricken, for example, are changing crops to those that can live on less moisture. "We first have to become a lot more efficient through methods like drip irrigation and growing crops that are more suitable to the local climate,"[27] says Sandra Postel. Organic farmers in areas that receive a lot of rainfall, on the other hand, often collect the rain using gutters or other methods and use it to help water their crops.

Organic farmers also experiment with new ways to conserve the water they do need. Planting crops on slight slopes, for example, allows water to trickle downhill to reach plants, which is more efficient than spraying water over a flat crop

Some farmers conserve and reuse water by collecting water already used for irrigation in tanks such as these.

surface. Organic farmers also use mulch (plant material like leaves and pieces of bark) or other ground cover to reduce evaporation, since soil that stays moist longer requires less-frequent watering.

Another method of conserving irrigation water is to reuse it. Organic farmers may collect water already used for irrigation and reapply it to the plants. Because chemical pesticides and fertilizers are not used on organic crops, the recycled water does not soak up many harmful chemicals and is safe to use more than one time. These are just some of the ways organic farms conserve the planet's limited freshwater while still growing food.

Soil Destruction

Farming practices can also destroy another critical resource for food production—the soil itself. Soil is a thin layer of material spread over most of the land on the planet. It contains small pieces of rock broken down over time by weather, but it also contains air, water, and decaying plant and animal matter. The combination of all four things makes soil capable of supporting plant life. Healthy soil gives a plant's roots the air, water, and nutrients they need and also anchors and supports them so the plant can grow tall. Not all soil is ideal for growing plants. The soil of deserts, for example, may be hard or sandy, lacking the water, air spaces, or dead plant and animal matter needed to grow new plants. Soil that is ideal for agriculture is actually a rather limited resource, but industrial farming practices can destroy the very soil they depend on.

Plants such as trees and grasses that grow naturally in an area are often removed so the land can be turned into farms. Soil with few to no plants growing in it has nothing to anchor it down. Wind and rain can then easily carry this loose soil away, similar to what happened when dry, bare soil blew away during the Dust Bowl of the 1930s in the American Midwest. The result is a landscape with thin or absent soil where plants might no longer be able to grow. This process is known as desertification, or the transformation of a once-fertile area into a desert-like landscape that lacks plant life.

When desertification happens, some farmers simply move on to another patch of land. This often means cutting down more forests or uprooting more naturally growing grasses to use the land for farming. This is especially a problem near rain forests in Africa, South America, and Asia. These forested areas have taken millions of years to grow and develop. When they are cut down for human agriculture, their soil may provide food for a season or two, but the plant and wildlife habitat they once supported may be destroyed forever. According to the United Nations Educational, Scientific and Cultural Organization (UNESCO), 24 billion tons of fertile soil is lost every year, carried away by wind and water when the climate and human activities both contribute to desertification. "Simply put, we take too much from the soil and don't put enough back,"[28] says sustainable agriculture expert John Crawford.

Improper farming practices can lead to soil destruction, as occurred during the Dust Bowl of the 1930s.

CHAPTER 4

Myths and Controversies About Organic Food

As the food-buying public learns more about the methods of industrial food production, people are becoming increasingly interested in organic foods. Some wish to avoid consuming foods grown in or with added chemicals from fertilizers, pesticides, hormones, and antibiotics. Others are concerned about the effects industrial farming is having on the environment and earth's natural resources. Some people merely wish to support small, local farms instead of industrial growers located far away, while others prefer the taste of organic foods or believe these foods provide better nutrition.

Whatever reasons people have for buying organic foods, they are doing so in greater numbers every year. Since 1999, the production of organic food worldwide has more than tripled, according to the International Federation of Organic Agriculture Movements. In the United States, organic products still remain a small portion of the total food industry, but American organic food production is predicted to grow by about 14 percent yearly through at least 2018. The Organic Trade Association estimates that as of 2014, more than 80 percent of American families bought organic products, especially fresh fruits and vegetables, at least some of the time. "The explosive growth in market share for organic produce in recent years testifies to a simple fact. . . . People don't like to eat food contaminated by pesticides,"[31] says Ken Cook, of the Environmental Working Group.

Despite this rapid growth in awareness of organic foods, many people are unaware of or uncertain about what organic food production actually involves. There are many misunderstandings and wrong assumptions about the organic food industry as well as about industrial methods of raising food. Knowing exactly what an organic food label means is important in helping people make smart decisions about the kind of food they eat and where they buy it.

What Organic Labels Mean

A majority of supermarkets and grocery stores now have designated areas for organic foods, especially in the produce section. Usually, there is a choice between fruits, vegetables, meats, and dairy products with a sticker that says

The Numi Organic Tea company has reduced its packaging in order to contribute less waste to landfills.

"certified organic" and products that do not have this label. A certified organic label guarantees the shopper that the foods were grown or raised on a farm that meets precise organic standards set and monitored by the USDA.

Farmers have the right to label produce and grain products as organic if they follow a list of restrictions that includes, among other things, not using synthetic fertilizers or prohibited pesticides on plants. Those who raise organic livestock must feed the animals certified organic food and cannot give them growth hormones or antibiotics. Organic farms must show that they are protecting natural resources, avoiding practices known to damage the environment, and using only fertilizers and pesticides that have been approved for organic foods.

Not all organic labels are equal. Foods in the produce, meat, and dairy sections are usually whole foods—those

Only products that meet precise organic guidelines set by the U.S. Department of Agriculture can be certified organic.

that do not have other ingredients mixed in. Much of the food sold in stores, however, has been processed, meaning things have been done to the food to change it from its natural state. Meats, fruits, and vegetables that have been frozen, dried, or canned are examples of processed foods. White baking flour is another example—wheat is ground into a fine powder and bleached to create this common product. Often, extra ingredients are added during processing, such as salt or sugar. Multiple ingredients also may be combined to produce things such as crackers, potato chips, and breakfast cereals.

Many processed foods have organic labels, but these labels can be misleading. An organic label on a piece of produce or a package of fresh meat means the product came directly from a farm that meets organic standards, but the same label on a processed, packaged

Organic Farming Worldwide

Supporters of organic farming believe industrial food production methods will eventually destroy the very resources people depend on to survive, but other people believe industrial farming methods are the only practical way to feed billions of people. In densely populated nations like China, for example, loss of a major crop could starve millions. Chinese farmers see chemical fertilizers and pesticides as crucial protection from underproductive crops. People across Africa, meanwhile, struggle with poverty and hunger and are unable to afford even industrially grown food, much less organic products that often come at an even higher price.

The immediate threat of starvation usually outweighs long-term concern about environmental damage. Even if organic farming becomes the norm in wealthier, developed countries like the United States, underdeveloped countries will likely still rely on whatever methods produce the most food—even if these practices come at a great cost to the environment. Doing otherwise could lead to widespread death and suffering. As the world's population continues to grow, finding sustainable ways to produce food for everyone could be humanity's greatest and most daunting challenge.

food only guarantees that 95 percent of the ingredients in the food came from organic growers. Up to 5 percent of the ingredients might not conform to organic guidelines. Confusing matters even more, some foods bear a label that says "contains organic ingredients." This merely means that at least one ingredient in the product was grown or raised by certified organic methods, and the label need not even indicate which ones. Many or even most ingredients in the product might not have been organically raised.

Other labels, such as "all natural" or "made with natural ingredients," may also mislead food shoppers. "Consumers

of any substance that is known to harm human health. If a chemical ever *is* proven to cause health problems, the FDA bans it from use in all American food. In this sense, the government considers any food grown on and sold from American farms safe to eat—organic or not.

In addition, although studies have shown that organic produce has from ten to a hundred times less chemical residue than nonorganic alternatives, the level of danger in nonorganic foods is nevertheless miniscule. "We have a tremendous amount of data showing that what we're exposed to in the diet for pesticides is very, very low, and certainly much lower than what would be required to have any even minimal health concern,"[34] says pesticide and risk assessment specialist Carl Winter.

The Truth About Hormones

Pesticide traces may be so small as to be called harmless by many food experts, but hormones used in beef, lamb, and milk products create a different consumer concern. Many people worry that the added growth hormones in meat and dairy products are building up in human bodies and causing health problems. Some people suspect growth hormones in animal products could be to blame for the phenomenon that modern children are entering puberty, the process of maturing into adults, an average of two and a half years earlier than children did in the 1950s, the decade hormones began to be used in American-grown livestock.

Growth hormones used on cattle and sheep are different than human growth hormones and therefore are unlikely to have a direct effect on people, but according to science and health journalist Carina Storrs, "The actual fear is that manipulating growth hormones in cows . . . may increase another hormone, insulin-like growth factor (IGF), which could mimic the effects of human growth hormone in harmful ways."[35] However, scientists say hormones used on dairy

Some farmers inject their cattle with hormones in order to increase the amount of meat they can obtain from the animal.

Unwelcome U.S. Foods

In 1988, the European Union—a political partnership between European nations—banned U.S. beef and dairy products from entering Europe because American farmers give hormones to their cattle. (Ironically, in 1989, the United States also banned European beef from being imported to the United States because of a European outbreak of mad cow disease, caused by a faulty component of a protein that can affect people's brains and nervous systems and cause death if they eat infected meat.)

Hormone-treated meat and dairy items are not alone among foods or food products the United States allows that other countries ban. Also included on many countries' banned lists are U.S.-grown chickens washed with chlorine or treated with a cancer-causing substance called arsenic to kill parasites. Farmed salmon, which are grown in captivity in the United States to reduce overfishing of wild salmon, make banned lists, too. The salmon are fed antibiotics, which turn their flesh a grayish color, so the flesh is then treated with chemicals to make it look pink, its natural color.

Despite other countries' refusal to import many food products from the United States, the American government states that none of these foods presents a real hazard to human health. American advocates of organic food, however, see such bans as justification for choosing organic products.

Many countries do not allow the import of chickens processed in the United States because of the use of chlorine or arsenic to clean the meat.

cattle break down in milk products to levels so low that they are barely greater than the amount of hormones in organic products—an amount that is still extremely small. "Just [to get] the amount of IGF secreted in your saliva and digestive tract in a day, you'd have to drink about 95 quarts of milk,"[36] says nutritionist Walter Willett.

Despite such assurances, many shoppers, especially parents, feel that hormone-free organic meat and dairy products are both safer and healthier. They wish to avoid any extra chemicals or hormones they fear might, over time, build up in the body and cause as-yet unknown effects on a person's health. "Today, we may be looking at environmental chemicals, steroids and so on that are causing puberty to begin in progressively younger kids," says pediatrician Susanne Tropez-Sims. "There's not been enough science to fully link hormones in the meat, but some of us are extrapolating that that's just what may be happening."[37]

Organic Food Is Not Automatically Healthy

The organic food industry only regulates chemicals and ingredients that are *not* allowed in food products. However, as organic foods become more widespread and popular, many consumers have come to believe that organic food actually has added nutrients that make it healthier than nonorganic choices. Some food manufacturers, even nonorganic ones, have begun to label their foods as being natural or containing organic ingredients in ways that seem to suggest these foods are more nutritious—or at least less unhealthy—than other foods. In most cases, this is untrue. Organic foods are not necessarily low in fat and calories, for example, nor are they guaranteed to be higher in vitamins and minerals than their nonorganic alternatives.

Some studies have shown that certain kinds of organic produce may have slightly more vitamins and minerals. One reason for this may be because organic products are often sold locally and have to travel for less time before reaching consumers in stores. Less travel time may result in slightly less breakdown of produce and its nutrients. Importantly, though, nonorganic foods do not lack nutrients that organic foods have. "We did not find strong evidence that organic foods are more nutritious or healthier than conventional foods,"[38] says Crystal Smith-Spangler, a medical researcher from Stanford University who participated in a 2012 study comparing foods grown with organic methods to those that were not. The notion that organic foods are vastly more nutritious than their nonorganic counterparts is a false one.

Just as an organic label does not guarantee that a food is more nutritious, it also does not promise that a food product is healthy. A pepperoni pizza, for example, may be made with organic meat, cheese, tomatoes, and crust, but it contains just as much fat and as many calories as a nonorganic pizza. Similarly, organic potato chips, cookies, and other snacks and desserts may still contain plenty of sugar, salt, and fat. Shoppers who purchase organic foods should not assume those foods are good for them just because of the organic label.

The public's confusion over what organic means and does not mean has worried many doctors and nutritionists. Shoppers may believe that only organic products are safe to eat and that other options might even be poisonous. However, the health benefits of eating fresh fruits and vegetables, whether organic or not, far outweigh any possible danger of pesticide exposure.

Shoppers who tend to avoid all produce because of concern about its safety put themselves at greater risk for future health problems such as cancer, heart disease, and strokes. People who do not eat produce are far more likely to succumb to these known killers than people who eat many fruits and vegetables, regardless of whether the produce is organic or not. "The average consumer doesn't think about that," says nutrition and internal medicine professor Carl Keen. "So I have concerns that he or she may shy away from consuming perhaps that apple, that banana, or that

Being labeled organic does not always mean a food is healthy because such foods may still contain high amounts of sugar, salt, and fat

pineapple out of a fear that it's unhealthy. What's occurring is they're making this trade off, they're not consuming it, which is quite bad in terms of their overall health, for a perceived risk that we can probably barely even quantify."[39] This is perhaps the most significant way the organic debate may be affecting the health of Americans.

A Genetic Alternative to Pesticides

As shoppers become wary of unknown chemicals leeching into their food, food growers face a dilemma. If they do not apply chemical fertilizers and pesticides, their plants may be weak and unproductive or may be consumed by unwanted invaders. If they do use synthetic products, however, they may damage the environment or grow food that people no longer want to buy. The answer, according to some botanists (plant scientists), is to learn to grow varieties of plants with the natural ability to do things such as ward off common pests, grow well with less water, or produce larger, sweeter, hardier fruits and vegetables without the use of fertilizers.

For centuries, scientists have tried breeding plant varieties with certain desirable traits and experimenting with the results. Successful modern ideas have included rice plants that can survive floods, a potato-like vegetable called cassava that is packed with a full day's supply of many critical nutrients, and papaya plants that are naturally resistant to pests. Such crops have the potential to help solve serious problems in the world. Cassava, for example, is an important crop for underfed people in Africa, and enriching it with extra nutrients can help ensure that people who only eat cassava can still get many nutrients, including protein, they otherwise would rarely be able to consume. Flood-resistant rice plants are important in places like Asia, where rice feeds billions of people and where a single flood could cause widespread food shortages and famine. Papaya, meanwhile, is vulnerable to many types of pests, and papaya crops are therefore heavily treated with pesticides. Hardier papaya plants would allow people to enjoy papaya that has been treated with few or no pesticides.

Cassava plants are naturally resistant to pests and are an important food crop for underfed people in Africa.

These are three examples of genetically modified organisms (GMOs), which have taken a large role in the organic food debate. To change or alter how plants grow and behave, scientists irradiate them, or expose them to radiation to alter their genes and give them new traits. By doing this, they create plants that are slightly different than non-modified versions. Even though *human* exposure to radiation can cause cancer in human cells, eating plant varieties whose ancestors' genes were at one time exposed to radiation has not been proven to cause cancer or any other negative health effects. Scientists worldwide, in fact, agree that GMOs are safe. According to the U.S. Academy of Sciences, "No adverse health effects attributed to genetic engineering have been documented in the human population," and the World Health Organization states that genetically modified foods "are not likely, nor have been shown, to present risks for human health."[40]

Nevertheless, many people, including many scientists, are not convinced that GMOs are entirely without risk. Because these products rely on scientific tampering, they may have unwanted and as-yet unknown effects both on people's health and the environment. For example, genetically modified plants growing in fields may pollinate natural varieties of the same plants growing close by, potentially resulting in unforeseen new versions or varieties that compete with the original species and may even cause them to die out. In addition, if scientists create GMOs that are resistant to pests, they may also contribute to the appearance of new insects, weeds, fungi, and other species that are hardier, too. If that happens, current pesticides may no longer work, and even more poisonous versions might have to be used.

The potential for such unforeseen consequences leads to uncertainty about whether GMOs are truly harmless. "Scientists who support transgenic crops . . . claim that the many GM crops that have passed safety tests somehow show that 'GMOs are safe,'" say the editors of the science journal *Nature*. "They should instead be giving the message that GM foods must be assessed on a case-by-case basis."[41] Because of such concerns, organic food guidelines in the United States currently prohibit organic farmers from creating, planting, or using GMOs.

The Future of Food

GMOs are yet another example of the many controversial issues facing the organic food industry. Nature, science, and business each have a large role in the growth and production of enough food to feed billions of people. Industrial farming methods have widespread negative effects on the world's natural resources—and, many people fear, on

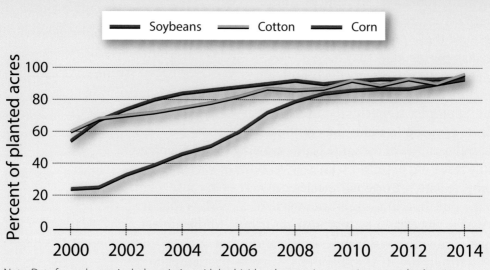

THE INCREASE IN THE USE OF GENETICALLY-ENGINEERED CROPS IN THE UNITED STATES

Soybeans —— Cotton —— Corn

Percent of planted acres

100
80
60
40
20
0

2000 2002 2004 2006 2008 2010 2012 2014

Note: Data for each crop include varieties with herbicide tolerance, insect resistance, or both traits.

Source: "Genetically Engineered Seeds Planted on over 90 Percent of U.S. Corn, Cotton, and Soybean Acres," United States Department of Agriculture Economic Research Service, August 7, 2014. www.ers .usda.gov/data-products/chart-gallery/detail.aspx?chartId=48577&ref=collection.

human health as well. Organic growing methods and the foods they produce are seen as a way to counteract these effects and are rapidly becoming more popular not just in the United States, but in countries around the world. The organic food market seeks to return, as much as possible, to natural methods of raising food.

Such techniques and practices take more time and more land, however. Industrial farming methods specialize in getting the most produce possible out of every farmable acre, whereas organic methods focus on a higher quality of food even if it means a smaller quantity. In many parts of the world, especially in highly populated areas such as much of Asia, organic methods may not be productive enough to feed everyone. When people must choose between feeding their family and supporting choices that are best for the environment, they are put in a difficult position. In many countries, organic foods and growing methods are considered a luxury.

Even in the United States, which has a much higher standard of living than many nations, people and families with a limited food budget may still question whether organic food is worth its usually higher cost or whether it is an extravagant purchase. Informed consumers make choices about the food they spend money on that are based on science and evidence rather than hearsay or misconceptions.

CHAPTER 5

Taking Part in the Organic Revolution

As organic products become more widely available, shoppers face an ever greater selection of food choices. Some grocery stores and supermarkets sell mostly or only organic products. Whole Foods Market, for example, was the first nationally certified organic grocer in the United States and has hundreds of stores in forty-two states, as well as the United Kingdom and Canada. Large retail chains such as Walmart, Target, Costco, Kroger, and Safeway carry an increasing number of organic options, too, usually offering specific aisles or sections of organic products to make it easier for consumers to find them.

More choices, however, can lead to confusion. Consumers spend time comparing products they plan to purchase, examining labels or appearances to determine how food items are different. They also compare price tags, and prices for organic products tend to be noticeably higher. Some shoppers misunderstand the price difference, assuming the higher cost of organic foods means they are superfoods packed with nutrients or health benefits other foods lack, even though studies have not proven this. Other shoppers shun organic food because they assume it always costs more, even though in some cases, organic options can cost the same as or even less than nonorganic alternatives.

Knowing what, when, and where to consider buying organic can help shoppers get the best nutrition for their money. People who understand what goes into their food, its packaging, and its price tag are better equipped to meet their nutrition goals, whether those include healthy eating on a budget, preserving the environment, or supporting food growers who live in their own community.

Organic Food Costs More

When compared side by side, organic and nonorganic produce usually is not visibly different, and it may be impossible for most people to tell organic and nonorganic meat, dairy, or grain products apart except for the label that says one is organic. Yet, the price of organic versions of foods can be anywhere from 20 percent to 100 percent more expensive. Because most of these products look and taste the same, some consumers wonder if they are merely paying more for a sticker or label. In fact, 59 percent of respondents in a March 2013 Harris Poll said they believed labeling foods as organic may just be an excuse for companies to charge more. "Many are wary of the 'greenwashing' concept that gives companies a chance to cash in on consumers who want to help the planet but are confused by all the eco-friendly jargon,"[42] says Harris Poll president Mike de Vere.

Government regulations prohibit grocers or food producers from using organic labels unless their foods meet organic standards, so customers can be assured that an organic label means something. The typically higher cost of foods bearing this label is in part related to the fact that meeting organic guidelines for food production requires more work. Industrial farming usually involves planting huge fields with a single type of plant, blanketing those fields with any pesticides necessary to keep damaging invaders out, using large machines to harvest and transport crops, and treating the soil with chemical fertilizers so that it can be replanted right away. Organic growers avoid most pesticides and chemical fertilizers used by industrial farmers and instead follow practices such as growing multiple types of crops on smaller pieces of land, pulling weeds by hand, letting soil recover between plantings, and fertilizing or controlling for pests with natural methods. All of this usually requires more labor and time, so many organic farmers must charge more for their products to make a living. "Time is money," says biologist Acata Felton. "Organic farms pay more in wages based solely on the number of person-hours invested."[43]

Organic foods usually cost more because they must follow strict guidelines such as not using pesticides.

Because organic farms rely more on natural than chemical or mechanical methods, they also tend to yield less produce per unit of land than industrial farms. Organic growers might lose one-third or more of a crop to invasive pests, for example. Their plants also tend to grow more slowly because farmers let them mature naturally instead of applying plant

hormones that force faster growth and ripening. Organic farmers do not plant genetically modified crops, either, which have been bred to do things such as repel pests or produce more food per plant. Altogether, organic farms tend to harvest and sell less food than typical industrial farms of the same size.

Organic poultry and livestock farmers also face challenges. They feed animals only organic food, for one thing, which costs more. They do not give growth hormones to cattle or sheep, as many industrial producers do, so animals raised organically grow more slowly, may be smaller as adults, and do not produce as much meat or milk as animals on conventional farms. Organic farmers also avoid giving antibiotics to animals unless they are sick, so they are at more risk of facing a disease outbreak among animals that could result in having fewer meat or dairy products to sell. Some organic farmers crowd fewer animals into an area, too, which is considered healthier and more humane for the animals, but which also leads to less food production than traditional livestock farmers can get by raising more animals on the same amount of land.

Organic products are generally in shorter supply than conventionally grown ones, but more consumers every year purchase organic foods. Thus, there is high demand for organic products even though supplies are low. Whenever there is a low availability of something many people want to buy, the cost of the product increases, a phenomenon economists call the law of supply and demand. This is something some stores also take advantage of. "To top it all off, the store may add a premium to the price of organics just because some consumers will accept the larger markup,"[44] Felton says.

For many reasons, organic food often costs more than food grown by conventional methods—but this is not always the case. "It's simply not as black-and-white as many people assume," says Charlotte Vallaeys, policy director of the Cornucopia Institute, an organic research and education organization. "On a price-per-ounce basis, heavily advertised

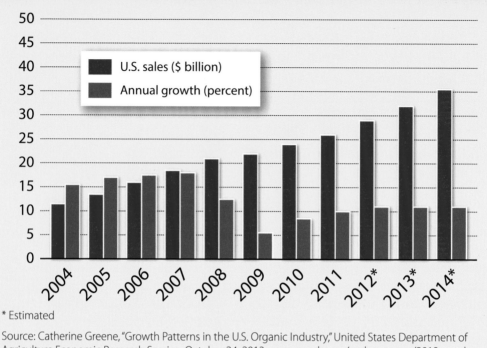

SALES OF ORGANIC FOOD IN THE UNITED STATES

Legend:
- U.S. sales ($ billion)
- Annual growth (percent)

* Estimated

Source: Catherine Greene, "Growth Patterns in the U.S. Organic Industry," United States Department of Agriculture Economic Research Service, October 24, 2013. ww.ers.usda.gov/amber-waves/2013-october /growth-patterns-in-the-us-organic-industry.aspx#.VFIAq7DF8rU.

brand-name foods from multinational corporations like Kraft and General Mills are often more expensive than wholesome organic equivalents that do not advertise and may require the occasional scooping, peeling or slicing."[45] Organic options can be affordable for most shoppers, especially if they know which organic products provide the best value and benefit for the money.

Dodging the Dirtiest

A main reason why people buy organic products is to avoid traces of chemicals in their food. They especially dislike the idea of consuming pesticides sprayed on fruits and vegetables and are willing to pay more to avoid them. Some fruits and vegetables tend to have more pesticides than others. A list called the Dirty Dozen names plants especially vulnerable to pests. To save these crops from being destroyed by weeds or insects, conventional farmers typically apply more pesticides. In 2014, the Dirty Dozen consisted of apples, strawberries, grapes, celery, peaches, spinach, sweet bell peppers, imported nectarines, cucumbers, cherry tomatoes, imported snap peas, and potatoes.

Most Dirty Dozen products test positive for traces of multiple pesticides, and apples are considered the dirtiest of the dozen; 99 percent of nonorganic apples test positive for traces of at least one pesticide. "The USDA washes and peels the produce items that it tests and they still find pesticide residues on 65 percent of the [Dirty Dozen] samples,"[46] says Alex Formuzis, vice president of the Environmental Working Group.

Spending more money for organic versions of Dirty Dozen foods seems worth it to many consumers, but these

Apples are considered the "dirtiest" food because 99 percent of nonorganic apples test positive for traces of pesticides.

crops are heavily treated with pesticides precisely because they are especially vulnerable to pests. Organic growers likely lose a portion of each crop to the same pests, resulting in less organic produce to sell and resulting in higher prices for it. Also, organic produce is not guaranteed to be entirely pesticide free, just to lack *certain* pesticides. Organic versions of the Dirty Dozen, although costly, may still be treated with some types of poisons.

Shopping Clean

Just as some crops are vulnerable to pests, others are naturally pest-resistant. These foods make another list called the Clean Fifteen because they are less likely to be treated with pesticides. In 2014, the Clean Fifteen included many fruits and vegetables with thick or tough rinds that are typically removed before eating, such as avocadoes, pine-

Foods in which the rind is not consumed, such as pineapples, are considered among the cleanest foods to eat.

apples, onions, mangoes, papayas, kiwis, grapefruit, and cantaloupe. Also among the Clean Fifteen were sweet corn, cabbage, asparagus, eggplant, cauliflower, and sweet potatoes, foods that seem to naturally ward off pests and are therefore treated with few poisons. Traces of pesticides on nonorganic foods like asparagus may be no higher, in fact, than on organic versions of these foods, so shoppers can save money by buying conventionally grown Clean Fifteen produce.

By purchasing any produce items they intend to peel, even those that are not Clean Fifteen products, shoppers can save money by buying conventional foods and still avoid some of the worry of consuming pesticides. "If you're going to eat the skin, consider organics," says registered dietitian Tanya Zuckerbrot. "But if you can peel the fruit or vegetable, you're going to strip away a lot of the residues anyway—so it's not really worth the extra money."[47]

Fresh Versus Frozen

The cost is not the only downside of purchasing organic fruits and vegetables. They also may not last as long as those that are conventionally grown. "Organic produce may spoil faster than conventional foods since they are not treated with waxes or preservatives,"[48] says registered dietitian Shanti Lewis. Organic foods' shorter shelf life (the amount of time it can remain uneaten without spoiling) may make them a less practical choice.

Frozen organic fruits and vegetables can help resolve this problem. Not only does frozen produce last a long time, it is also considered a healthy alternative to fresh produce because it is frozen immediately after being harvested. The longer a fruit or vegetable has been separated from the plant on which it grew, the more nutrients it loses, so produce frozen soon after picking is preserved at the peak of nutrition. One food on the Clean Fifteen list, in fact, is frozen sweet peas. For consumers who are wary of added chemicals in their food but are unable to shop frequently for fresh items, frozen organic produce can be a practical and affordable alternative.

Teenagers Take to the Farm

Every summer in Boulder, Colorado, kids and teens ages twelve to nineteen run and manage their own organic farm through Cultiva, an urban agriculture youth project. Participants spend ten to fifteen hours a week planting, nurturing, and harvesting produce they then sell at farmers' markets. "It's an intense experience with all kinds of plants—fruit, root, and leaf crops," says 2014 Cultiva participant Christopher Kiley. "We learn not just how to grow but how to harvest and sell these foods."

The program teaches leadership and job skills, but more importantly, participants learn to value the environment and to support natural ways of growing food. "Agriculture is becoming a lost art," Kiley says. "We need to help our community choose fresh foods, not simply what you can buy in a package."

Cultiva is one of many programs that involve young people in the organic food industry. A growing number of 4-H chapters offer organic food programs, and organic farms may hire teen work crews or offer summer camps or apprenticeship programs. Many colleges and universities also offer opportunities through agricultural extension programs. The National Institute of Food and Agriculture provides Internet links to such programs for each state at www.csrees.usda.gov/qlinks/partners/state_partners.html.

Quoted in Radha Marcum. "Can Organic Farming Turn Around At-Risk Teens?" *Organic Connections*, June 29, 2014. www.organicconnectmag.com/organic-farming -turnaround-troubled-teens.

Organics in the Meat and Dairy Aisle

Organic meat and dairy foods are at least as popular as organic produce. Many consumers are willing to spend more money to buy organic than conventionally raised animal products, especially to avoid the possibility of consuming extra hormones they fear could lead to health problems. As with produce and pesticides, however, people who do not fully understand organic livestock laws and practices can be misled about what they are paying for and why.

In the United States, farmers are only allowed to give hormones to cattle and sheep. Nevertheless, some sellers of products in which hormones are prohibited, especially poultry, add noticeable labels to packages to state that the meat they contain is hormone-free. Consumers may falsely believe these products are different or better than the competition, sometimes even paying more for them. "These poultry production claims are often relatively meaningless," says organic meat farmer David Maren. "They're designed to paint a picture of what the customer wants to buy without requiring significant changes in the . . . poultry production model."[49] Informed consumers do not pay more for chicken or pork just because the label states the obvious fact that these products are hormone-free.

Beef and milk products are different. Since American farmers are allowed to give hormones to cattle, products labeled as having no added hormones are different than products from hormone-treated cattle. Still, hormone-free is different than organic. Organic meat and dairy products are hormone-free, too, but they also come from animals that are given all-organic feed. Consumers who pay for truly organic meat and dairy foods avoid not just the added hormones, but the possibility of pesticide residue built up in the tissues of the animal products they consume.

Faced with so many choices, shoppers are often unsure what to buy. Some fear that buying anything but certified organic products in the meat and dairy aisles amounts to poisoning themselves and their families. Others continue to purchase conventionally raised and lower-priced products because they are unconvinced that eating hormone-treated or nonorganic meat and dairy products causes any negative health effects.

Many nutritionists and physicians point out that the known dangers in animal products are not hormones at all. "Cholesterol, fat (especially saturated fat), and animal protein are the major culprits in meat that are associated with higher risks of heart disease, diabetes, and some cancers," says the

Physicians Committee for Responsible Medicine. "While concentrations of some contaminants may be decreased, switching to organic meat does nothing to decrease the risk for the diseases that remain the biggest killers of Americans."[50] Many health experts advise people to buy and eat fewer animal products overall, which will also cut down on the risk of exposure to added hormones, whether the products are organic or not.

Processed Foods

Processed foods that are labeled organic, such as this macaroni and cheese, may contain a mix of organic and nonorganic ingredients.

Organic products take up an increasing amount of shelf space outside of the produce, meat, and dairy aisles, too. Breads, cereals, rice, and pasta are processed foods among which organic versions are now common. Such products are made from grains, and most organic-minded consumers wish to avoid eating pesticides that were applied to the wheat, corn, oat, and rice crops before they were harvested, ground into flour, and used in other products.

Many packaged foods, from breakfast cereals and bread loaves to granola bars and spaghetti, now come in organic versions, usually with a higher price tag. Such foods may contain a mix of organic and nonorganic ingredients, however, so shoppers committed to an all-organic diet must read labels carefully to know what they are actually buying.

Snack foods is another grocery category where organics are gaining shelf space. One advantage organic snack foods may have over their nonorganic competitors is that they tend to contain fewer chemical ingredients overall. Organic snack foods are more likely to leave out certain preservatives, food colorings, and other things that may be found in similar but nonorganic foods. "People want to know what's in their food," says Illinois chef and restaurant owner Jared Linn. "They don't like going to the grocery store and reading the back of a can and seeing 95 ingredients . . . and not knowing what 93 of them are."[51] Many consumers choose to spend more on organic packaged products simply because the ingredient list contains fewer unrecognizable things. More nonorganic food packagers are also making changes to exclude things such as dyes and additives, however, so organic products may not always be significantly different.

Commonsense Ways to Eat Healthy for Less

Many studies about the lifelong health benefits of organic foods (or about health problems that might be caused by eating nonorganic foods) are inconclusive. Organic foods are not proven to save lives, and conventionally farmed foods are not proven to endanger them. The choice to eat organic foods, conventional ones, or a mix of the two is personal, and there are many ways for people to build a healthy diet.

> ## NUTRITION FACT
> ### 9
> As the first digit on four-digit product lookup (PLU) code on produce, indicates an organic item. For example, a conventional banana's PLU code is 4011, while an organic banana's is 94011.

Grow Your Own Organic Food

The only sure way for people to know exactly what has gone into their food from soil to harvest is to grow it themselves. Gardening is a growing trend and has the added benefit of providing low-cost, healthy produce. Some people have plenty of space outdoors to create large gardens with everything from fruit trees to rows of corn and squash, but a small backyard also provides plenty of space to grow many edible plants. Even people who live in urban apartments or townhomes can grow a variety of foods. Tomatoes, herbs, and peppers, for example, grow well in containers that can fit on most apartment balconies or even in a windowsill where they have access to sunlight.

People who want to grow larger plants or crops but lack the space can also start or join a community garden, which is owned and operated by a group of people who rent or buy plots of land where they can grow their own fruits and vegetables. Many high-rise apartment buildings have gardening areas on their rooftops, making it possible for people in the city, not just in the country, to experience growing, harvesting, and eating their own food.

A sure way for people to know that they have the healthiest fruits and vegetables is to grow them themselves.

People who do worry about pesticides in their produce can lessen their exposure to them just by following common nutrition advice to eat a wide variety of fruits and vegetables. Farmers, both organic and conventional, tend to treat different types of plants with different pesticides based on the particular pests that afflict them. Therefore, eating a variety of produce not only gives people a wider variety of vitamins and minerals, it lessens the chance of being exposed to large amounts of any one type of pesticide, whether a person buys organic fruits and vegetables or conventional ones.

Simple habits like rinsing produce also go a long way toward reducing pesticide residue. Pesticides build up on the outer surfaces of fruits and vegetables, so washing or rinsing them can cut residue traces by as much as 50 percent. Buying in-season produce that is grown close by is another way to reduce exposure to extra chemicals in food. The farther food has to travel from where it is grown to where it is sold, the more preservatives and chemicals may have to be added so it does not spoil before it reaches consumers. Most fruits and vegetables also grow better during certain seasons, so when farmers grow produce outside of its normal season, they often have to use extra fertilizers or hormones to coax the plants into growing. Such produce may also have to travel a long distance, since many plants grow only in warmer climates during winter months and need to be shipped to shoppers who live in colder places.

Buying seasonal produce grown on nearby farms is an easy way to spend less money on healthy foods, especially organic ones. "The closer the source, the fresher the food," say nutrition experts Jonny Bowden and Jeannette Bessinger. "Choosing seasonal foods is both inexpensive [foods in season are plentiful, so they tend to run lower in cost than the rest of the year] and healthy [foods harvested and eaten at the peak of their growing season are the richest in nutrients]."[52]

The Global Impact of Organic Food

Supporting local farmers is not only a good way to find food with fewer chemicals, it may have positive effects on the environment, too. Reducing the distance food products must be shipped results in using less fossil fuels and causing less air pollution. Small local farmers, many of which produce organic foods, may not be able to compete with larger commercial farms in stores around the country and do not grow or raise enough food to be able to afford shipping and processing costs. They can, however, afford to sell their products in their own communities. Local farmers' markets are often convenient places to buy high-quality produce, even organic varieties, at a lower cost than at many supermarkets and grocery stores.

Purchasing foods from local farmers' markets is a good way to support organic farmers, get healthy foods, and have a positive impact on the environment.

Buying locally may benefit shoppers, food growers, and the environment at the same time. Small, local, organic farms tend to actively preserve soil, waste less freshwater, and reduce pollution. Many people believe industrial farming methods have pushed traditional, natural farmers to the brink of extinction, but with the renewed support of customers in their own communities, many local farms are able to stay true to their organic roots.

As the human population continues to grow, however, industrial farming will continue to be a major force in world agriculture. Organic methods, although they benefit both human health and the environment, may not be able to keep up with the endlessly growing demand for food. On the other hand, conventional farming methods may also eventually destroy the resources needed for food to grow. The most important question about organic farming may be whether its environment-friendly methods can grow enough to feed the world at prices people can afford. It is an issue that affects food growers and shoppers not just in the United States, but everywhere. The organic and conventional food industries will likely need to work together to meet what has always been and will continue to be the human race's biggest challenge—obtaining food.

Chapter 1: Food for a Modern World Returns to the Old Ways

1. Tom Standage. *An Edible History of Humanity*. New York: Walker, 2009, pp. ix–x.
2. Standage. *Edible History of Humanity*, pp. ix–x.
3. Amy Bentley and Hi'ilei Hobart. "Food in Recent U.S. History." In *Food in Time and Place: The American Historical Association Companion to Food History*, edited by Paul Freedman, Joyce E. Chaplin, and Ken Albala. Oakland: University of California Press, 2014, p. 171.
4. Melanie Warner. *Pandora's Lunchbox: How Processed Food Took over the American Meal*. New York: Scribner, 2013, p. 61.
5. Paul B. Thompson. *The Agrarian Vision: Sustainability and Environmental Ethics*. Lexington: University Press of Kentucky, 2010, p. 49.
6. Franklin D. Roosevelt. "Statement on Signing the Soil Conservation and Domestic Allotment Act." March 1, 1936. Available at University of California, Santa Barbara, American Presidency Project. www.presidency.ucsb.edu/ws/?pid=15254.
7. Paul K. Conkin. *A Revolution Down on the Farm: The Transformation of American Agriculture since 1929*. Lexington: University Press of Kentucky, 2008, p. 97.
8. Quoted in Helena Bottemiller. "Pesticide Residue Rankings: Apples and Celery Worst, Onions and Corn Best." *Food Safety News*, June 19, 2012. www.foodsafetynews.com/2012/06/in-pesticide-residue-rankings-apples-and-celery-worst-onions-and-corn-best/#.VCTNUxYXOkI.

Chapter 2: Organic Food and People's Health

9. Gerald G. Moy. "Risk Analysis: Chemical Hazards." In *Encyclopedia of Food Safety*, edited by Yasmine Motarjemi, Gerald Moy, and Ewen Todd. Waltham, MA: Academic Press, 2014, p. 93.
10. Mark Drewes, Klaus Tietjen, and Thomas C. Sparks. "High-Throughput Screening in Agrochemical Research." In *Modern Methods in Crop Protection Research*, edited by Peter Jeschke,

Wolfgang Krämer, Ulrich Schirmer, and Matthias Witschel. Weinheim, Germany: Wiley-VCH, 2012, p. 3.

11. Sameeh A. Mansour. "Pesticide Residues in Man." In *Pesticides: Evaluation of Environmental Pollution*, edited by Hamir S. Rathore and Leo M.L. Nollet. Boca Raton, FL: CRC Press, 2012, p. 469.

12. Quoted in Jesse Hirsch. "Farm Confessional: Secrets of a Supermarket Produce Buyer." *Modern Farmer*, January 22, 2014. www.modernfarmer.com/2014/01/farm-confessional-supermarket-produce-buyer.

13. Anna Neumeier. "Granulation Opens Opportunities in Precision Agriculture." FEECO International blog. www.feeco.com/granulation-opens-opportunities-precision-agriculture.

14. Sam Angima. "Toxic Heavy Metals in Farm Soil." *Oregon Small Farms News*, published by Oregon State University, vol. V, no. 3, Summer 2010. http://smallfarms.oregonstate.edu/sfn/su10toxicmetals.

15. Dan Charles. "A Mixed Blessing." *National Geographic*, May 2013. http://ngm.nationalgeographic.com/2013/05/fertilized-world/charles-text.

16. Joan Yau. "What Are Plant Growth Regulators?" *Food Safety Focus*, July 2011. www.cfs.gov.hk/english/multimedia/multimedia_pub/multimedia_pub_fsf_60_02.html.

17. Rita Klavinski. "7 Benefits of Eating Local Foods." Michigan State University Extension, April 13, 2013. www.msue.anr.msu.edu/news/7_benefits_of_eating_local_foods.

18. U.S. Meat Export Federation. *USMEF Factsheet: Hormones*. Denver: U.S. Meat Export Federation, November 2007. www.usmef.org/downloads/07_1015_Hormones Factsheet.pdf.

19. Renu Gandhi and Suzanne M. Snedeker. "Consumer Concerns About Hormones in Food." Fact Sheet #37. Ithaca, NY: Cornell University Program on Breast Cancer and Environmental Risk Factors, June 2000, updated 2010. www.envirocancer.cornell.edu/factsheet/diet/fs37.hormones.cfm.

20. Testimony of Dr. Stuart B. Levy before the Subcommittee on Health of the U.S. House Committee on Energy and Commerce, July 14, 2010. www.tufts.edu/med/apua/policy/7.14.10.pdf.

Chapter 3: Organic Food and the Environment

21. Quoted in Andrew Giambrone. "Current Farming Practices Unsustainable, Expert Says." *Yale Daily News*, September 15, 2010. www.com/blog/2010/09/15/current-farming-practices-unsustainable-expert-says.

22. Steve Wing. "Environmental Injustice Connects Local Food Environments with Global Food

Production." In *Local Food Environments: Food Access in America*, edited by Kimberly B. Morland. Boca Raton, FL: CRC Press, 2014, p. 65.

23. Robert H. Friis and Thomas A. Sellers. *Epidemiology for Public Health Practice*, 5th ed. Burlington, MA: Jones & Bartlett Learning, 2014, p. 559.

24. Quoted in Megan Noe. "Sales from Organic Farms Spike in Illinois." WQAD 8 News, May 7, 2014. www.wqad.com/2014/05/07/sales-from-organic-farms-spike-in-illinois.

25. Elisa Lanzi. "Impacts of Innovation: Lessons from the Empirical Evidence." In *Encyclopedia of Energy, Natural Resource, and Environmental Economics*, edited by Jason F. Shogren. Waltham, MA: Elsevier, 2013, p. 83.

26. Quoted in Brian Handwerk. "Sustainable Earth: Water." *National Geographic* website. http://environment.nationalgeographic.com/environment/sustainable-earth/water.

27. Quoted in Handwerk. "Sustainable Earth."

28. Quoted in World Economic Forum. "What If the World's Soil Runs Out?" *Time*, December 14, 2012. http://world.time.com/2012/12/14/what-if-the-worlds-soil-runs-out.

29. Quoted in World Economic Forum. "What If the World's Soil Runs Out?"

30. Quoted in Kate Bertrand Connolly. "New Ways to Green Your Food and Beverage Packaging." *Food Processing*, December 20, 2012. www.foodprocessing.com/articles/2012/green-your-packaging.

Chapter 4: Myths and Controversies About Organic Food

31. Quoted in Bottemiller. "Pesticide Residue Rankings."

32. Quoted in Mike Hughlett. "Food Makers' 'Natural' Claims Draw Scrutiny." *Star Tribune*, March 2, 2014. www.startribune.com/business/248044731.html.

33. Quoted in WFTS Tampa Bay. "No Testing Procedures in Place to Assure Organic Produce Is Chemical-Free, So We Tested Ourselves." ABC Action News, February 24, 2013. www.abcactionnews.com/news/local-news/i-team-investigates/no-testing-procedures-in-place-to-assure-organic-produce-is-chemical-free-so-we-tested-ourselves.

34. Quoted in Melinda Wenner Moyer. "Organic Shmorganic." *Slate*, January 28, 2014. www.slate.com/articles/double_x/the_kids/2014/01/organic_vs_conventional_produce_for_kids_you_don_t_need_to_fear_pesticides.2.html.

35. Carina Storrs. "Hormones in Food: Should You Worry?" *Huffington Post*, January 31, 2011. www.huffingtonpost.com/2011/01/31/hormones-in-food-should-y_n_815385.html.

36. Quoted in Storrs. "Hormones in Food." Brackets in original.

37. Quoted in Katti Gray. "Hormones in Food May Lead to Early Puberty." *The Grio*, February 12, 2013. www.thegrio.com/2013/02/12 /hormones-in-food-may-lead-to -early-puberty/2.

38. Quoted in Alice Park. "Is It Worth Buying Organic? Maybe Not." *Time*, September 4, 2012. www .healthland.time.com/2012/09/04 /is-organic-food-more-nutritious -and-healthier-than-conventional -varieties.

39. Quoted in Bottemiller. "Pesticide Residue Rankings."

40. Quoted in Michael White. "The Scientific Debate About GM Foods Is Over: They're Safe." *Pacific Standard*, September 24, 2013. www .psmag.com/navigation/health -and-behavior/scientific-debate -gm-foods-theyre-safe-66711.

41. "Poison Postures." Editorial. *Nature*, September 25, 2012. www.na ture.com/news/poison-postures -1.11478.

Chapter 5: Taking Part in the Organic Revolution

42. Quoted in "Majority of Americans See Organic Label as an Excuse to Charge More." Harris Interactive, April 15, 2013. www.har risinteractive.com/NewsRoom /HarrisPolls/tabid/447/ctl/Read Custom%20Default/mid/1508 /ArticleId/1180/Default.aspx.

43. Acata Felton. "Is Organic Produce Worth Your Hard-Earned Green?" *Stanford Alumni*, January/February 2012. https://alumni.stanford .edu/get/page/magazine/article /?article_id=46697.

44. Felton. "Is Organic Produce Worth Your Hard-Earned Green?"

45. Charlotte Vallaeys. "The Cost of Organic Food Is Worth It and—Surprise—It's Not Always Higher." *Cornucopia News*, October 23, 2013. www.cornucopia.org/2013 /10/busting-organic-expensive -myth.

46. Quoted in Jessica Firger. "Pesticides Aplenty in Your Fruits and Veggies: The 2014 'Dirty Dozen.'" CBS News, April 29, 2014. www.cbs news.com/news/pesticides-aplenty -in-your-fruits-and-veggies-the -2014-dirty-dozen.

47. Quoted in Sunny Sea Gold. "Is 'Organic' Worth It?" *Men's Fitness*. www.mensfitness.com/nutrition /what-to-eat/is-organic-worth-it.

48. Shanti Lewis. "Is Organic Really Worth It?" *Baltimore Sun*, July 10, 2012. http://articles.baltimoresun. com/2012-07-10/health/bs-fo -nutrition-organic-20120710_1 _organic-food-organic-farmers -organic-ingredients.

49. David Maren. "What You Should Know About Poultry Production Claims." *Mark's Daily Apple*, June 4, 2014. www.marks dailyapple.com/what-you-should -know-about-poultry-production -claims/#axzz3EwsJiuCg.

50. Physicians Committee for Responsible Medicine. "Organic Meats Are Not Health Foods." www.pcrm.org/health/health-topics/organic-meats-are-not-health-foods.

51. Quoted in Noe. "Sales from Organic Farms Spike in Illinois."

52. Jonny Bowden and Jeannette Bessinger. *The 150 Healthiest Comfort Foods on Earth*. Vancouver, British Columbia: Fair Winds, 2011. Kindle version.

GLOSSARY

antibiotic: A drug or substance used to kill harmful bacteria.

biodegradable: Capable of being broken down by nature, bacteria, and other means of decay.

compost: Decayed plant material used to improve soil for agriculture.

desertification: The process by which land becomes a desert through climate, human activity, or both.

famine: A situation in which many people do not have enough food.

fertilizer: A substance added to soil to help the growth of plants.

genetically modified organism (GMO): A living thing whose genes have been altered by genetic engineering processes.

irradiation: Exposure to energy produced by radioactive substances or nuclear reactions.

organic: Food grown or made without artificial chemicals.

pesticide: A chemical used to kill animals, insects, or plants that damage crops.

plant growth regulator (PGR): An organic compound, either natural or synthetic, that modifies or controls biological processes within a plant.

Center for Food Safety

660 Pennsylvania Avenue SE, #302
Washington, DC 20003
phone: (202) 547-9359
fax: (202) 547-9429
website: www.centerforfoodsafety.org

This nonprofit organization promotes safe, sustainable, and environmentally sound food systems to protect human health and the environment. It monitors the agricultural industry, both organic and conventional, for violations of food safety and environmental laws.

Ecological Farming Association (EcoFarm)

2901 Park Avenue, Suite D-2
Soquel, CA 95073
phone: (831) 763-2111
e-mail: info@eco-farm.org
website: www.eco-farm.org

This organization focuses on bringing people together through education and communication to create a healthful food system that strengthens soil, protects air and water, and honors rural life.

Organic Consumers Association (OCA)

6771 South Silver Hill Drive
Finland, MN 55603
phone: (218) 226-4164
fax: (218) 353-7652
website: www.organicconsumers.org

This nonprofit organization has more than 800,000 members, subscribers, volunteers, and advocates for food safety, health, environmental sustainability, and related topics.

Organic Crop Improvement Association International (OCIA)

1340 North Cotner Boulevard
Lincoln, NE 68505-1838
phone: (402) 477-2323
fax: (402) 477-4325
e-mail: info@ocia.org
website: www.ocia.org

This nonprofit organization is one of the world's oldest, largest, and most trusted leaders in the organic certification industry. It provides research, education, and certification services to organic growers, processors, and handlers worldwide.

Organic Trade Association (OTA)

28 Vernon Street, Suite 413
Brattleboro, VT 05301
phone: (802) 275-3800
fax: (802) 275-3801
website: www.ota.com

This organization, founded in 1985, is the business association for the organic industry in North America and helps advocate for and protect organic regulations and standards to give consumers confidence in organic products.

Sustainable Food Trade Association (SFTA)

49 Race Street
New Castle, VA 24127
phone: (413) 624-6678
e-mail: info@sustainablefoodtrade.org
website: www.sustainablefoodtrade.org

This nonprofit organization focuses on fair selling and trading for organic food producers, encouraging strong business practices for organic products from farm to retailer.

U.S. Department of Agriculture (USDA)

1400 Independence Avenue SW
Washington, DC 20250
phone: (202) 720-2791
website: www.usda.gov

The USDA is the federal agency that oversees the American agriculture industry and provides leadership on agriculture, nutrition, natural resources, and providing food for American citizens and others around the world.

U.S. Environmental Protection Agency (EPA)

1200 Pennsylvania Avenue NW
Washington, DC 20460
phone: (202) 272-0167
website: www.epa.gov

This agency of the federal government writes regulations and enforces laws Congress passes to protect human health and the environment. One of its primary issues is regulating pesticides in food and water and educating the public about pesticide dangers.

Books

Jeff Gillman. *The Truth About Organic Gardening: Benefits, Drawbacks, and the Bottom Line*. Portland, OR: Timber Press, 2008. From the history of organic gardening to pest control, fertilizers, and environmental effects, horticulture professor Jeff Gillman takes an objective look at organic food and its pros and cons.

Jennifer Landau. *Incredibly Disgusting Environments: Pesticides and Your Body*. New York: Rosen Publishing Group, 2013. Myths and realities of agricultural pesticides and their true risk for human and environmental health are examined.

Andrew Langley. *Is Organic Food Better?* Chicago: Heinemann Library, 2009. This book discusses major controversies in organic food, including its impact on health, animals, and the environment.

Alex Mitchell. *The Edible Balcony: Growing Fresh Produce in Small Spaces*. New York: Rodale, 2012. An experienced urban gardener gives advice on how to grow produce even in the city, using small spaces ranging from apartment balconies to rooftop gardens.

Kimberly Lord Stewart. *Eating Between the Lines: The Supermarket Shopper's Guide to the Truth Behind Food Labels*. New York: St. Martin's, 2007. This grocery-shopping guide describes what goes into everything from produce, meat, and dairy to processed and packaged foods, including what labels mean and how to understand them. Readers will learn how to make more informed choices about what they buy and eat, whether the products are organic or conventional.

Articles

Mary Beth Albright. "Organic Foods Are Tastier and Healthier, Study Finds." *National Geographic*, July 14, 2014. http://theplate.nationalgeographic .com/2014/07/14/organic-foods-are -tastier-and-healthier-study-finds. Discusses recent research suggesting that organic foods have both nutrition and taste advantages over conventional foods.

David Biello. "Will Organic Food Fail to Feed the World?" *Scientific American*, April 25, 2012. www.scientificameri can.com/article/organic-farming -yields-and-feeding-the-world-un der-climate-change. Discusses concerns that current organic growing methods alone cannot produce enough food to sustain the world's population and advocates a blend of organic and conventional methods.

Aaron Carroll. "Is Organic Food Better for You?" CNN, August 5, 2014. www.cnn.com/2014/08/05/opinion/carroll-organic-food-nutrition. A pediatric medicine professor sorts through the claims of organic and conventional farmers to sort out the facts and myths about health benefits of organic foods.

Websites

Center for Ecoliteracy (www.ecoliteracy.org). This site contains several resources for rethinking school lunches and encouraging students, teachers, and communities to make school foods healthier, more natural, and more friendly for the environment.

Mother Earth News, Organic Gardening (www.motherearthnews.com/organic-gardening.aspx#axzz3FW16rrgb). The organic gardening section of Mother Earth News's website has articles, videos, a blog, and other features to help private gardeners grow their own food organically.

Organic Agriculture, U.S. Department of Agriculture (USDA) (www.usda.gov/wps/portal/usda/usdahome?navid=organic-agriculture). This section of the USDA website is dedicated to organic agriculture. It describes the federal standards for organic food products, and has information on conservation, organic research and education, and more.

Organic Foods at Helpguide.org (www.helpguide.org/articles/healthy-eating/organic-foods.htm). This searchable site provides information on many basic questions about organic food, including labeling, costs, health benefits, and facts about organic meat, dairy, and produce.

U.S. Agricultural Marketing Service's list of U.S. certified organic producers (http://apps.ams.usda.gov/nop). This site contains a database of more than twenty-seven thousand companies and producers worldwide, updated yearly, that meet the standards for U.S. certified organic products.

INDEX

F

Farmers' markets, 85–86, *86*
FEECO International, 31
Fertilizers
    on organic foods, 58, 60–62
    overview, 30–33, *32*
    pollution by, 47–48
    use in China, 59
Food for modern world
    changing nature of, 17–18
    chemical cutbacks, 24–26
    food safety, 20–22, *21*
    history of food laws, 18–20
    onset of agriculture, *14*, 14–15
    overview, 13–14
    shipping food supplies, *10*, 15–16
    World War II impact, 22–24
    See also Organic food
Food laws, 18–20
Food safety, 20–22, *21*, 60–62
Food shortages, 19, 67
Fossil fuel pollution, 44–46, *45*

G

Garbage disposal concerns, 54–55
Genetically modified organisms (GMOs),
    67–69, *68*, *70*, 75
Gibberellin hormone, 33–34
The Grapes of Wrath (Steinbeck), 23
Growth hormones
    bovine growth hormone, 37, 38–39
    livestock with, 36–39
    meat and dairy foods with, 36, 37, 81
    truth about, 62–65
    use of, 33–36, *35*, 60, *63*
Gulf of Mexico dead zone, 50, *50*

H

Heavy metal buildup, 31–33
Herbicides, 28

I

Industrial Revolution, 16
Industrialized farming
    agricultural practices, 44, 73
    benefits of, 70
    harm from, 59
    introduction, 9–10
Insulin-like growth factor (IGF), 62,
    63–64
International Federation of Organic
    Agriculture Movements, 56
Irish potato famine, 19, *19*
Irrigation
    agricultural practices, *47*, 47–48
    conservation efforts, *51*, 51–52
    runoff water, *47*, 48, 49
    with wastewater, 50

J

The Jungle (Sinclair), 23, *23*
Just Label It, 60

L

Labeling myths with organic food, 57–59,
    58
Ladybugs, 30, *30*
Livestock industry
    antibiotic use, 39
    cattle industry, 36, 64
    changes to, 24
    hormone use, 36–39, 62
    organic challenges to, 75
    organic laws for, 58, 60, 81
    pollution from, 44
    poultry industry, 39, 64, *64*, 75
    water runoff from, 49

M

Malaria, 43
Meat industry, 80–82

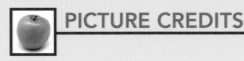
PICTURE CREDITS

Cover: © Alison Hancock/Shutterstock.com, © Goran Bogicevic/Shutterstock.com, © wavebreakmedia/Shutterstock.com

© Allstair Scott/Alamy, 35

© Chicago Tribune/Getty Images, 57

© CSU Archives/Everett Collection, Inc./Alamy, 53

© Dana Hoff/Bon Appetit/Alamy, 58

© Edwin Remsberg/Alamy, 64

© Egon Zitter/Shutterstock.com, 47

© Enigma/Alamy, 11

© Everett Collection Historical/Alamy, 21, 23

© Fotokostic/Shutterstock.com, 28

© Gale, Cengage Learning, 70, 76

© George Rose/Getty Images, 25

© Graphic Science/Alamy, 30

© Ian Shipley IRE/Alamy, 19

© Ilya Frankazoid/Shutterstock.com, 32

© JLPH/Cultura RMAlamy, 74

© kezza/Shutterstock.com, 51

© mangostock/Shutterstock.com, 86

© Mathisa/Shutterstock.com, 78

© NASA/RGB Ventures/SuperStock/Alamy, 50

© Newscast/Alamy, 17

© Nigel Cattlin/Alamy, 40

© Nitr/Shutterstock.com, 77

© Patti McConville/Alamy, 82

© photogal/Shutterstock.com, 10

© Picsfive/Shutterstock.com, 45

© Sayan Puangkham/Shutterstock.com, 68

© Tony Hertz/Alamy, 63

© unchalee_foto/Shutterstock.com, 14

© vivver/Shutterstock.com, 84

© Whitebox Media/Mediablitzimages/Alamy, 66

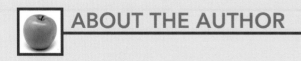

ABOUT THE AUTHOR

Jenny MacKay is the author of more than twenty-five books for teens and preteens. She grew up in a farming community in northern Nevada, where crop dusters, cows, and tractors were familiar sights, but her family grew their own fruits and vegetables. She still lives close to her childhood home with her husband, son, and daughter.